LOVE
&
MARRIAGE

BOOK ONE

THE LOVE STORY OF

NANCY & FRANK

NANCY LOU HENDERSON

NLH PRESS

LOVE & MARRIAGE
Book One
The Love Story of Nancy & Frank

© 2019 by Nancy Lou Henderson

www.NancyLouHenderson.com

 facebook.com/nancy.henderson.39

 twitter.com/nlhende49

NLH Books

ISBN 978-17938718-6-2

Printed in the United States of America.

Dedication

to frank

Table of Contents

1

love begins

My family, the Blakleys, moved to Van Vleck, Texas in the summer of 1966. My parents, Jim and Mary Blakley, were teachers.

I was one of five children, the only girl, and if you were going according to the pecking order, number two. I would be a junior in high school in the fall of 1966.

Frank had lived in Van Vleck, Texas and in Sugar Valley, a little community about three miles outside of Van Vleck, for all but a couple of years of his life. Frank was the son of Loren and Peggy Henderson. Frank was the oldest of three children. He had one brother and one sister. Although we were the same age with only thirty hours difference in our births, Frank would be a senior in the fall of 1966. Frank had attended a private kindergarten then was allowed to skip the first grade in Van Vleck Elementary.

Frank and I would have only one class together during that school year which consisted of both juniors and seniors. The class happened to be a chemistry class taught by, none other than, my mother. I sat at a long table with other junior girls and Frank sat at a table with senior boys. Thinking back now, I am not sure that was such a great ideal to have all of those guys at one table. Frank and his buddies' table was to the right and a little to the rear of the table that I sat at with the other junior girls. When my mother's back was turned from the class as she wrote on the blackboard, Frank would throw spit wads at me but since I knew he had a steady girlfriend, I would just ignore him.

One day as I got up to walk to the front of the class to ask my mom a question, upon returning to my table, Frank told me that I had great legs. I did not even look up to acknowledge him as I sat down in my chair. *What was he thinking?* I remember thinking to myself that he had a girlfriend. Back in those days you just did not talk to other girl's boyfriends. The strangest thing about him saying that to me is that I remember him saying it to me after all of these years. It is amazing how the little things stay in your mind.

The fall, winter, and spring of the 1966-1967 school year passed quickly but other than sharing that class with each other, Frank and I would not date, but in the summer of 1967, Frank and his longtime girlfriend would go their separate ways.

In the fall of 1967, I would be a senior in high school and Frank would enter Wharton County Junior College as a freshman. My oldest brother, Jimmy, would also attend WCJC along with Frank and some of his friends. They would all carpool together to save gasoline. Frank would come to our house every morning of the weekdays to either pick Jimmy up or to leave his car and ride with Jimmy. It seemed like Frank was always at our house for breakfast on school days.

Frank and Jimmy had met in the summer when Jimmy had gotten a job helping Frank and his dad haul hay. Frank's dad owned hay trucks and for a second income he would haul hay which gave Frank and his brother plus many others jobs in the summer.

The fall of my senior year I was on the Annual Staff and my job was to take pictures during sporting events so I would be on the football field every Friday night. Frank and Jimmy were also on the football field running the down markers and chains for the coaches. Frank would constantly make remarks to me such as "You missed a great picture" or "Did I tell you, you have nice legs?"

At the time I really just wanted to smack him with my camera but then when I would look at him, he had such an amazing smile with the biggest dimples I do believe I had ever see seen and I also knew that he did not have a girlfriend any-more which made me a lot more interested in him as a dateable guy. Funny how fast news travels in a small town when a guy or girl is free-grabs for dating.

As the school year progressed, Frank and Jimmy became best friends and Frank was always at our house nearly seven days a week. When they were not in school, they were hanging out on Friday and Saturday nights together at our house, eating our food and getting ready to go to a dance somewhere to check out girls or maybe drink a little, make that a lot, of beer. They had another friend who was always with them who had graduated with Frank. I called the three of them "The Three Musketeers."

One Saturday after lunch, I was in the kitchen at my folk's house washing dishes when I suddenly heard a voice right behind me, asking me if I was getting the dishes clean. After turning around, I saw Frank standing there smiling. I told him, of course, I was getting the dishes clean but that if he thought he could do a better job to have at it. He just smiled then told me he thought I was doing an awesome job. There was a brief silence as he just stood there staring at me then he asked me if I would like to go out with him sometime if Jimmy and their other friend got a date.

I looked at him for a moment studying his face trying to figure out just what he meant when I told him sure if your buddies get a date we will go out sometime. Frank smiled at me then turned and walked back into the den where my brother and his other buddy were hanging out.

Thinking about Frank, I finished the dishes then was headed to my bedroom when the phone rang. Since the den was only divided from the kitchen by a bar which had stools around it for eating, just sitting or visiting, when the telephone rang which hung on the wall above the bar, I stopped to answer the phone.

It was a male friend of mine from high school asking me for a date to the drive-in that evening. I told him it sounded like fun then he told me he would pick me up about 7:00 that evening. I hung up the phone and started walking through the den towards the hall which led to my bedroom but as I was passing the Three Musketeers, they started to harass me, telling me that Frank had asked me out first, and then I had accepted a date with someone else. I tried to defend myself by explaining that Frank did not ask me out that very night but it was to no avail. They were in true harassment mode.

I finally just left the room laughing knowing they were not about to stop, plus I had to shower, wash my hair, roll it on rollers and then dry it. I showered, got dressed and then headed to my room to roll my hair then dry it under the hair dryer when here they came. They stood there watching me roll my hair, telling me how badly I had hurt Frank's feelings and what a terrible person I was. I just laughed at them and kept rolling my hair knowing I could not wait to get under that hair dryer so I could not hear them anymore.

Finally, they exited my room and I quickly got up from my dressing tabled then locked the bedroom door. When my hair was dry, I put on my makeup, took out the rollers, and brushed my hair. I waited in my room until it was time for my friend to arrive then ran quickly to the front door and out to his car, jumped in and told him to drive. I had escaped "The Three Musketeers."

My date and I drove to Bay City, Texas, a town about three miles from Van Vleck, purchased a soft drink at Cains Drive-in, and drove to the Showboat Drive-in movie, which was about halfway between Bay City and Van Vleck. We drove around inside until we found a good place to park the car then removed the speaker from its pole and my date placed it on his window which he had rolled halfway down. We sat there talking, drinking our soft drinks, and waiting for it to get dark enough so the movie could begin.

Suddenly, I noticed a car driving slowly down the road in front of the aisle we were parked on and without a doubt, I realized it was the Three Musketeers. Immediately, I knew this was not going to be good! They drove past us then drove down the road behind us.

Of course, the Three Musketeers pulled into the aisle right behind us, started flashing the lights of my brother's car, yelling out of the windows, then they decided to get out of their car, come to the windows of the car we were sitting in and started knocking on the glass.

Since they were obviously very drunk, I told my friend that I thought it would be best if we just left and he drove me home. I could see by the look on his face that he thought that was a great ideal. He tossed the speaker out of the window, started the car, and quickly we drove out of the drive-in. When we got to my house, I told him thank you, jumped out of the car, then told him to drive quickly away from my house before I ran into the house.

My dad was sitting on the couch in the den when I entered the house through the garage which had a door that opened near the bar that led into the den. The garage door opened right before the bar on the den-side. Dad looked up from the show he was watching on television then told me that I was home really early from my date. I told him that the movie was not really very good then I headed down the hallway to my bedroom. Suddenly, I stopped for a moment in the hallway when hearing a car screeching to a halt in our driveway. Immediately, I knew who it was and exactly how drunk they were. So, I just walked right on into my bedroom, sat down at my dressing table, started brushing my hair and waited for the fireworks to begin!

I heard Frank and Jimmy enter the house through the garage door laughing loudly and definitely still quite drunk. From my room, I could hear dad ask them if they had been drinking. Frank just laughed loudly as Jimmy told dad that they had not.

Hearing dad and Jimmy getting into a serious discussion, looked up to see Frank entering my bedroom from the hall. Frank plopped down on my three-quarters bed, which had wooden slats to hold up the boxed springs, then the mattress, Frank, and the boxed springs went crashing to the ground.

Frank acted like nothing had happened at all while he was laughing loudly telling me that "they were drunk as skunks" and that Jimmy was trying to tell my dad that they had not been drinking!

I was mortified, then told Frank that he needed to get out of my bedroom before my dad caught him in there. Frank got up from the bed but as he was leaving the room, he told me, "Nancy, you are my girl and nobody dates you but me. We're going out tomorrow night."

I told him, "Okay, Frank. Please leave my bedroom now."

I knew that if my dad caught him in my bedroom Frank would be a "dead" date. Actually, I believed the next day he would not remember our entire conversation but there was something about that smiling drunk face with those incredible dimples made me hope that he would remember.

The next morning Frank called and apologized for his behavior the previous evening then asked me if I would consider going out with him that night. I told him that I would but we would have to go to MYF which was Methodist Youth Fellowship and then to church afterward.

Frank humbly agreed to my request then he told me he would pick me up at 5:45 p.m. I was really excited about seeing him again. Something about Frank just made my heart flutter like never before. That smile, those dimples, the sound of his voice and the way he looked at me with his beautiful eyes as if I was the most beautiful girl in the world. I would have to guard my heart when I was around him — but did I really want to?

Frank arrived right on time to pick me up and we had also made plans to double date with my brother and my best girlfriend after church. The next morning at church, I told my girlfriend about what had happened the night before. She and I came up with a "get you back" plan. We were electing new officers at MYF that evening, so we decided to put Frank in for president and Jimmy in for vice-president. We let all of the other MYF members in on our plan and that evening they were elected. Frank looked at me when they won then he just winked at me to let me know he knew what I had been up to.

After MYF and church were over, we all piled into Jimmy's car and drove to Bay City with Frank and me in the backseat and Jimmy driving with my girlfriend sitting next to him in the front seat. We were driving through town making the drag down the main street when Frank asked Jimmy if he knew what their other buddy, the third Musketeer, was doing.

Jimmy told him, "No, I don't."

Frank thought we should drive by their buddy's uncle's house to see what he was up to, so of course, we did. Jimmy stopped the car when we got there then he and Frank got out of the car and went inside. They told us that they would just be gone a minute. Fifteen minutes passed by but they had not come back, so I looked in the front seat and saw that the keys were still in the ignition.

I told my girlfriend that we were going for a drive, then I got out of the car, opened the driver's door, and got in the car then started the car and off we drove. They really should not have left the keys in the car! I drove us to a hangout place on the main street of the town called Cains. It was a drive-in where you could get food and drinks with a carhop named Mary.

We ordered two cherry Dr. Peppers which came with a little plastic animal on the side of the cups. We sat there until fifteen minutes before we were supposed to be home then drove back and picked up the two Musketeers we had abandoned.

Jimmy and Frank got in the car but we had decided not to talk to them. Half way to Van Vleck, Frank asked me if I was upset with him, then pulled me close to him but before I could answer, he kissed me. Oh my gosh, I knew immediately I was hook, line, and sinker in love with him. My heart was pounding, I couldn't breathe much less think. I looked at Frank then he smiled at me which did not help but increased what I was feeling. How could I be in love with Frank after just one kiss?

Thank goodness we were finally pulling up to the parking lot of the church where Frank's car was parked. Frank and I got out of Jimmy's car then into Frank's car and drove to my house. Frank and I didn't talk, just sat there driving in silence. When we got to my house, Frank walked me to the door. When we reached the front door I turned to tell him goodbye but Frank took me in his arms and kissed me again then told me that he was in love with me and I knew that it was true. I told him that I was in love with him too. There really was not any doubt that we were in love and we both knew it.

Frank turned to leave but turned back and told me, "Nancy, I am going to marry you."

I replied to him, "I know, Frank."

I watched him get into his car and drive off wondering, *What the heck just happened?* From that night on, I was the fourth Musketeer, Frank and I were inseparable, very in love, and we went everywhere together.

2

the hayride

A s president of the MYF (Methodist Youth Fellowship), Frank decided to plan some fun events for us all. Since Frank's dad owned hay trucks, Frank decided it would be fun to have a hayride.

After borrowing his dad's hay truck, Frank loaded it with bales of hay placed around all sides, so everyone could sit on top of the bales then lean back on the sides of the truck. Frank got in the truck and then headed to my house to pick me up then we drove to the church to pick up all of the other MYF members.

When we arrived at the church everyone was anxiously waiting then climbed on board the back bed of the truck, sat down then Frank and I got back into the cab to the truck. Frank was the driver and I was his passenger "shotgun."

After the MYF members, their friends and dates were loaded securely on the truck, Frank drove the truck across town and then turned on to Old Van Vleck Road. We had only gone only about two miles when the skies opened up and it started to rain. Frank found a place to pull the truck into then turned the truck around and headed back to the church driving as fast as he could.

When we arrived at the church all of the passengers in the back of the truck quickly unloaded then ran into the church. Frank turned to me then told me that the hay was going to get wet and asked me if it would be alright if he backed the hay truck into my parent's garage. I told him that I thought it would be okay with them. My parents had gone out of town but would be back later in the evening but I knew that they would not mind.

Frank and I headed to my folk's house that was only about eight blocks from the church. When we got to the house the garage door was open. Since it was a two-car garage with only one door, Frank backed the truck onto the driveway then started to back into the garage.

After Frank's door cleared the garage door opening, he opened his door a little to look back as he backed the truck into the garage because he could not see through the back window of the truck because the stacked hay got in the way of the rear view mirror.

When Frank had backed in as far as he thought enough so as not to hit the back wall, he opened the door all the way until it was touching the wall on his side of the garage. Frank turned off the ignition then took his foot off of the clutch. Suddenly the truck jumped backward and the open door stuck into the sheetrock wall that the door was touching.

Oh, my goodness! I was horrified. My parent's house was not even a year old and now we had put a hole in the sheetrock in the garage. Frank looked at me and he could see the panic on my face. Frank smiled at me then calmly took my hand then told me, "Nancy, I promise you, I will fix it."

Frank and I got out of the truck and pulled the door out of the sheetrock then shut the driver's side door then we went into the house to wait for my parents to return home. Frank and I sat on the couch then he tried hard to make small talk with me but all I could think about was that hole in the sheetrock and I was trying not to cry.

Finally, the time passed by and we heard my folk's car drive up outside. Of course, the rain had stopped about two minutes after the catastrophe to the sheetrock. Frank met my folks at the door and told my dad what had happened to the wall in the garage, then he told dad that he would return the next morning to fix the wall. Frank apologized for what had happened. Dad accepted his apology, they shook hands, and dad told Frank he would see him the next morning.

Frank returned the next morning with sheetrock, sheetrock tape, nails, paint and any other tools he would need to fix the wall. Frank fixed that wall and it looked like nothing had ever happened to it. I was so proud of him. I was reminded again how much he owned my heart and I knew my heart would have to continue to grow to hold all of the love I would have for him in it.

Frank gave me his high school ring to wear on my hand after our first date. I would wrap white surgical tape around and around the backside of the ring until it would fit my finger then paint the tape with fingernail polish, which made the tape look really awesome. This was how we wore our boyfriend's ring in the high school I went to in 1968.

Frank and I were doing everything together. He would pick me up, take me to school, and then pick me up after school. I could not wait to see him every morning and after school. I could tell that he felt the same way.

My senior year was becoming the best year of my life. Frank and I would go on dates but nothing expensive because I knew that he was paying for his own college. He would ask me if I wanted to go out to eat but I would tell him I just wanted to be with him and I did not need to go out to eat and spend his hard-earned money.

Our dates usually consisted of Frank picking me up at my house then we would drive into Bay City, stop at Cains to get a cherry Dr. Pepper, sit there visit with our friends for a while then we would make the main drag in town with the windows down listening to Frank's eight-track player playing his tapes which were usually The Righteous Brothers who were Frank's favorite group.

Of course, we would also listen to the radio with all of the popular songs in the summer of 1968 then if a good movie was playing at the Showboat Drive-in movie we might go there. If we did go to a movie, we would always go to a store first and buy two cans of black olives to eat at the movie because we both loved black olives.

3

new year's eve

About a month or so after our first date and during our Christmas break, Jimmy, Frank, and I were invited to a New Year"s Eve 1967 party in Houston, Texas which was at my cousin and her husband's house.

We left Van Vleck and all went to my cousin's home, together in my brother's car. My cousin and her husband already knew Frank because they had met him at my grand-father's funeral in December, so no introductions would be needed. After we arrived at the party everyone was already in party mode and munching on snacks that my cousin had provided for everyone. The room was full of music and laughter.

Frank and I decided that we would go into the kitchen get some food and fix us something to drink. There was a lot of food on some of the counters but one counter held nothing but different kinds of sodas, condiments like candied red cherries, lemon slices, lime slices, green olives and many bottles of different kinds of liquor.

I was eighteen but I had never drunk a mixed drink or beer. Drinking just was not something girls did back then that I knew in the town where I lived. Guys, on the other hand, seemed to drink beer, a lot of beer. I told Frank that I was going to make myself a mixed drink. Frank asked me if I wanted him to make it for me but I told him no I would do it myself. After all, how hard could it be? Frank kind of laughed but told me to go ahead.

After picking a large glass, I poured some of all of the liquors in the glass until the glass was about two-thirds full, then I poured some of each kind of soft drink and finished it off by adding at least one of each condiment. Wow, that drink looked awesome!

Frank asked, "Nancy Lou are you going to drink that?"

I replied, "Of course, I am. Frank, would you like me to fix you a drink just like mine?"

Frank told me he thought he would wait a while. So, I took a big drink of my mixed drink which tasted really wonderful. I really loved the taste of my mixed drink, so I took another big drink. Frank was watching me, then he told me that I might want to drink my beverage a little slower. Smiling at him, I told him that I knew what I was doing and anyway it tasted really great.

Frank and I walked back into the living room where everyone else was gathered then sat down on the couch. Wow, I felt good but it had gotten really hot in there. The music was playing loudly and I just wanted to dance, so I got up off of the couch, stepped up onto the coffee table and danced! I was even singing! I felt so free and alive!

Frank got up off of the couch and put his arms around my waist then lifted me off of the table. After my feet back were back on to the floor, Frank took my hand, led me through the kitchen then out the back door of the house to the backyard.

My cousin's backyard sat next to a drive-in theatre. The only thing that separated her backyard and the drive-in was a fence. Wow! I could see the movie playing on the big screen, so I took off running for the fence and proceeded to climb it! Frank was running behind me laughing then he pulled me off the fence before I could climb over it.

As he placed my feet back on the ground, I realized I was getting really dizzy and my legs felt really wobbly. Suddenly, Frank picked me up in his arms and carried me into the house but unfortunately that was the last thing I remember.

I have heard stories of other things I might have done but then again, I claim innocence of those stories because I do not remember. The next thing that I do remember was Frank holding my hair back from my face while my cousin held a cool rag on my forehead as I was hanging my head over the toilet while sitting on the floor gagging and feeling like the contents of my stomach would never stop emptying.

I do remember my cousin telling Frank that she thought it would be best if he, Jimmy, and I just spent the night at their home and she would call my parents. At the time I did not know that Jimmy was also passed out on the couch very drunk.

My cousin called my folks and told them that it was really late and she thought that because there would be many drunks on the road that we should just spend the night at her house. My folks did not fall for it and told her we should drive on home. Of course, my cousin did not mention that two of us were hopelessly drunk and we would be the drunks driving on the road.

Frank loaded Jimmy into the backseat of the car then he carried me to the car then put me into the passenger side of the front seat. I was literally in and out of consciousness. Frank, who was a person who did not know a lot about driving in Houston and was directionally challenge, climbed into the driver's seat, started the car, then we were on our way into the night.

Jimmy was passed out asleep in the back seat but I kept tapping Frank on the shoulder so he would stop the car so I could open my door to mainly dry heave. The trip home should have taken us only an hour and a half but with Frank losing his direction and me making him stop the car, it took us three-and-a-half hours.

I do not remember getting to my house, getting out of the car, getting undressed or into my bed that night, but I do remember waking up in the morning with an awful headache.

For some strange reason, my folks were not upset with me the next morning but did seem to be enjoying my suffering a lot.

My basketball coach, who lived next door to my folks, came over to tell me that he had called a special practice for that afternoon, then he laughed as he looked at me while telling me about it.

Well, I went to that basketball practice that afternoon and the coach ran my booty off, yo-yo after yo-yo!

Frank called earlier in the day and came over to my house to check on me that evening. He told me it might just be better if I did not drink and I told him I totally agreed.

4

a long way home

One night after Frank and I left Cains where we had sat and visited with our friends, he asked me if I wanted to take a different road on our way back to Van Vleck to take me home.

Frank told me it was a shell road and it was a nice scenic drive, which would take us a back way into Van Vleck. Something told me told me that maybe Frank had something more on his mind than looking at the scenery, especially since it had been raining and there was a creepy fog hugging the ground which made it hard to see anything.

I told Frank, "I don't think we will be able to see anything with the fog."

Frank smiled that big smile of his, then replied, "Yes, Nancy, it is foggy but we can still see the stars."

I replied, "Really Frank? We are going stargazing?"

Frank did not answer but was just smiling with his dimpled face looking at me when I agreed to his new route. Dang those dimples! Frank knew that I trusted him with my heart and I knew I could trust him to go stargazing but besides that, I knew that I could handle him. So, we turned off of highway 35 on to another road which led us to turn on to a shell road.

The fog was now creeping along the ground and was about halfway up on the sides of the car. It was very thick and it looked like we were driving through a cloud. We could barely see the road in front of us.

Frank had his left hand on the wheel, his right arm wrapped around me, the music was playing loudly and we were cruising along in his car when suddenly water was rushing on to the hood of the car then the car died.

I thought, *Oh, my goodness! Did we drive into a lake? Where was the road?*

All I could see around us was fog and water, lots and lots of water. Of course, back in this day and time, we did not have cell phones. Frank and I were definitely "up a creek without a paddle" — or a running car.

Frank rolled up his pants legs, took off his shoes and socks, opened the door then got out of the car. Frank walked to the front of the car and opened the hood then after a few minutes he closed the hood. Frank walked back to the car and got back inside.

Frank looked at me smiling then said, "Nancy, I have good news and bad news. The good news is that the water isn't really very deep and the car is sitting on a bridge that crosses a creek. The bad news is that the spark plugs on the car got wet so we will have to stay here for a while until they dry out so the car will start."

All I could think of as Frank told me the bad news was that I had a curfew and my Dad was never going to believe this story, ever! I reminded Frank of my curfew then he just smiled and told me, "Nancy, just look how beautiful the stars are."

I was thinking, *Are you kidding me, Frank? stars?*, then I told him, "Frank, you need to get this car started now and take me home before my curfew or my dad is going to shoot us both."

Well, that did not work for me because Frank decided that he would just be "Mister Funny Man"! Frank got out of the car, walked through the water, climbed up on the hood, stood there with his hand in a salute and looking side to side like he was in a crow's nest on a ship. Of course, I could not stop myself from laughing which was exactly what he knew I would do.

Suddenly, out of the fog, a truck appeared in front of us. A rice farmer got out of his truck and told "Hood Dancer" Frank that he had witnessed us stop abruptly and knew that we had probably stalled out in the water which was running over the bridge because of the rain we had received during the week.

The man had brought a chain with him to pull us out of the water, which he did, and then he helped Frank get the car started. Frank and I thanked the man then we were off cruising in the car again.

Frank was back to his left hand on the wheel, his right arm wrapped around my shoulders, the music was playing loudly and we were cruising down the road again.

Frank was looking at me smiling with those big dimples when he said, "I told you it would all be okay, Nancy. Just look at all of those stars in the sky in front of us as we are driving."

I just smiled back at him knowing that the light that shone in him and from him was brighter than any star in the sky

Frank and I made it to the door of my house with minutes to spare before my curfew ended. He gave me a big hug with a long kiss standing on the porch of my folk's home and I did not seem mind that at all.

It seemed like things were moving so quickly in our relationship but it also seemed like we had known each other our entire lives. We were alike but different; we strengthened each other's weaknesses and together had doubled our strengths.

God definitely had a plan for us to become one. December had come to an end and it was the middle of January. Frank and I had been together as a couple for about a month and a half but it seemed like we had known each other all of our lives.

Frank was on Christmas break from college still but I was not on break from high school and I was playing basketball. Frank would come to all of my practices and watch us practice then try to show me after practice how to do a hook ball but to no avail, because I was a guard, shooting baskets was just not my forté.

Frank had played football, ran track, and played basketball in high school. He loved sports, so he loved watching me play basketball and trying to help me improve.

Frank bought me a beautiful gold ID bracelet for Christmas with his name engraved on it. It was my first gift from him and I still have it.

5

february 7, 1968

I n mid-January 1968, Jimmy and Frank were supposed to register to go back to school at Wharton County Junior College but after talking with the registrar and my dad, they decided to enlist in the Army.

It seems that they had been spending more time drinking Tall Boy beer and playing pool at a place nearby the college than going to classes. Their grades had also suffered badly. Since going to college and making good grades was their only deferment from being drafted, it was in their best interest to just join the Army.

Frank and Jimmy went to a recruiter to talk to him about their best choices. The recruiter talked them into joining the ASA, Army Security Agency, for four years. He promised them that they would never go to Vietnam because the ASA was not in Vietnam, which was a total lie. The recruiter also told them that they would be on the Buddy System which meant where ever one of them went the other would also go, which would also be proven to be untrue. Frank and Jimmy signed the papers and then went home.

When Frank got to his house, he called me and asked me if I would like to go out to eat that night. I told him yes but that we did not have to go out to eat because I knew he had just spent money on tuition at the college. He told me that he wanted to take me out somewhere nice to eat. I told him that was nice and I would go.

Frank picked me up at about 7:00 that evening and we drove to Bay City to a favorite restaurant that we both liked. We ate and just enjoyed being together. When we finished eating, Frank paid the food bill and we walked hand in hand to his car. After we got into the car and drove out of the parking lot, Frank told me he would like to go somewhere quiet where we could be alone together and talk. He drove us to a small park in town then turned off the car. I could see when I looked into his eyes that he had something bothering him. We sat there in silence for a minute.

Then Frank said, "Nancy, I enlisted in the Army today."

My heart sank and I was trying hard to fight back tears. My head was swimming in total confusion with thoughts. Was the love of my life breaking up with me? Had I been a complete fool? How could I ever live without him?

So many emotions were flooding my mind with so many questions when I finally had to know the answers.

I took a breath trying to hold back the tears, then I timidly asked him, "Frank, what about us?"

Frank pulled me close to him, cupped my face in his hands, looked into my eyes and kissed me. When our kiss ended Frank told me, "Nancy, we are getting engaged before I leave for basic training and then after basic training, I am coming home and we are getting married then you are going to go with me where ever I go. I love you with all of my heart and I can't live life without you, Nancy."

Frank kissed me again and I felt like I was absolutely floating on a cloud! God had definitely given me such a wonderful gift! I was going to be Frank's wife and I could not ever have asked for anything better. Frank and I were true soulmates. Our love for each other was true and deep.

We were both eighteen years old and only thirty hours separated the days of our birth. Frank was born late at night of October 4, 1949, and I was born on the morning of October 6, 1949. I am not sure if this is what made our connection so strong but I do know that in the future it would become even stronger and amazing things would happen between us.

I have no doubt that God intended on us to become one heart and soul. This all happened on February 7, 1968.

Frank told me that he had not told his parents yet about him joining the service or his plans for us but would tell them the next day. We talked some more about the future then just sat there looking at the stars and being in love.

Frank told his parents the next day, February 8, 1968, that he had joined the Army and then he told them that he was getting married. I had not formally met Frank's folks as his girlfriend but I knew them from our church. Frank had always told them when he left to go out at night that he was going to Jimmy's house. Frank's folks did not have a clue that he was dating Jimmy's sister. So, when Frank told his folks he wanted to get married his dad asked him, "Frank, who are you going to marry, Jimmy?"

Frank then explained to them that he had been dating me. I am sure that it was quite a shock for them but then again everything he told them that day was a shock! Since Frank's folks had married at our age and his Dad was in the Army at the time, they understood what was in his heart and agreed to us getting married.

My folks, on the other hand, knew that we had been dating since late November of 1967 but I was still in high school and would finish my Senior year the end of May 1968. I had been accepted into The University of Texas and I was also accepted into a sorority dorm on campus, so us getting married might just be a problem. Everything was moving really fast but so was the love in our hearts.

Frank called me and asked me for a date that same night. Frank picked me up and then we went for a drive. Frank wanted to talk to me about asking my Dad for my hand in marriage and he was a little nervous about it. Dad already knew that Frank had joined the Army, so I told him to just ask my dad.

Then Frank asked me, "Nancy, what if he says no?"

I told Frank, "Mom and dad love you and dad is not going to say no. We are both eighteen years old, we can make this decision for ourselves and they know that."

Frank seemed to be less worried then but still had some doubts. It was still early so Frank looked at me then said, "Let's go do it, Lou."

Frank smiled at me and I returned his smile. After all what could happen? Frank and I drove to my house. When we arrived, we got out of the car, walked through the garage and entered the house through the garage door which led into the kitchen. I really thought that Frank would actually squeeze my hand off as we walked holding hands through the garage!

Frank and I said hello to my parents and then sat down at the bar. I sat on a stool facing the kitchen and Frank sat directly across from me on the kitchen side of the bar on a stool facing the den. On Frank's right side was the kitchen stove. Dad was sitting on the couch in the den which faced the kitchen. He could see Frank sitting on the stool in the kitchen. Mom was ironing clothes close to the bar.

Frank was really nervous and was leaning back on two of the legs of the stool he was sitting on rocking back and forth. I looked at Frank who was looking very pale and smiled then without speaking tried to encourage him to speak by mouthing to him without words, "Do it, Frank. What are you waiting for?"

Frank was looking at me and leaning back on two legs of his stool when he suddenly blurted out, "Mr. Blakley, what do you think about Nancy and I getting married?"

There was a brief silence in the room and then Dad rose from the couch looked at Frank and said loudly, "Frank, I don't think a damn thing about it!"

Frank, who was rocking back and forth on his bar stool, fell over backward, hit the side of his head on the stove handle and fell to the kitchen floor!

I sat there horrified thinking, *What just happened? Is Frank okay?*, when dad started laughing loudly and ran over and helped Frank up off of the floor.

Dad told Frank that it was okay for us to get married and then shook Frank's hand. What Frank did not know was that I had already told dad that Frank had asked me to marry him the night before. I told dad that I was in love with Frank and I also told dad that Frank would be asking him if I could marry him soon.

My dad was a jokester and he decided to play a joke on Frank. Dad and mom loved Frank and he had already become a part of our family. My folks could see the love Frank and I had for each other and the love Frank had for all of my family.

I thought to myself, "Who wouldn't love this freckled faced dimpled cheeked guy?"

The next night Frank's folks invited me to come to their house for supper. It was my turn to be nervous. I could not seem to find the right dress to wear, the right shoes and my hair just would not do the right thing. I was a nervous wreck.

Finally, the time for Frank to pick me up came and we drove to his folk's house. When we arrived, Frank and I got out of the car, walked to the front door and he opened the door so we could go into the house. Frank's mother had heard our car drive up outside and met us in the hallway.

Then she walked up to me and put her arms around me then said, "So, you are Nancy. Welcome to our home, Nancy, and welcome to our family."

I was instantly in love with her and she had removed all of my fears then the three of us walked into Frank's folk's den where his dad sat.

Frank's dad got up from his chair, came over to me, and hugged me then said, "Glad to meet you, Nancy, and it is always a pleasure to meet all of Frank's girlfriends."

My mouth instantly gapped open in surprise but then He immediately started laughing and Frank laughed with him. I knew then that my dad would not be the only jokester in our family.

We had an awesome supper sitting around their dining room table then I helped Frank's mom clear the table and wash the dishes while Frank and his dad went into the den then when Frank's mom and I finished the dishes, we joined Frank and his dad in the den.

We had so much fun just talking and getting to know each other. About 10:00 p.m., Frank and I said our goodbyes and we left so he could take me home.

On the drive to my house, Frank told me that the next morning he would like to take me to Bay City to look at engagement rings. He said that his mom had asked him if she could go with us but he wanted to ask me first before giving her an answer. I told him that it was definitely all right with me for his mom to go with us but I really did not need a ring to know I was engaged to him.

Frank just smiled his big dimpled face smile then said, "Nancy, that's one reason I love you but I want a ring on your finger saying you are all mine and not available to anyone else."

I was thinking as I smiled back at him, *I will never be anyone else's but yours with or without a ring on my finger. I would even wear a rubber band. You are my heart and soul, my forever love.*

I told him, "Frank, I love you and you own my heart forever."

The next morning, which was February 10, 1968, Frank and his mom picked me up at my house and we drove to Bay

City. We went to a jewelry store named Secrest, which was on one side of the square across from the County Courthouse. Frank's parents had known the Secrest family for many years and that made picking out a ring so much more personal and special.

Frank kept showing me these beautiful rings, which had large diamonds, but I had already spotted the ring that was perfect. It was very dainty with a small diamond set on a slightly raised setting with two small diamond chips on either side of the diamond. The wedding band had three diamond chips evenly spaced on the top of the ring. Since I had small delicate hands and I liked delicate jewelry, I asked Frank if the ring described above could be my ring.

Frank just smiled at me, then said want, "Nancy, I want you to have any ring you want but please don't worry about the cost."

I told him, "Frank, this is really the ring that I want."

Frank's mom looked at me with the biggest smile. I guessed that she liked the ring too. Of course, Frank told me it was okay and then the jeweler measured my finger to get a ring size which size of 5½. The jeweler told us it would take a few days to get the ring sized.

Frank's mom suggested that we might want to go ahead and pick out china, pottery, drinkware, stainless steel silverware and real silver silverware. She told us that more than likely there would be several wedding showers and it would be nice for people to have suggestions or things we might like to have.

We did what Frank's mom suggested and we had so much fun. Frank and I both loved roses, so everything had roses of some kind on it. Frank let me pick the color of the roses on the china and pottery, so the roses were a delicate light pink.

On February 14, 1968, which was a Wednesday, Frank picked me up from my house to go out for Valentine's Day. We went out to eat and then he drove to our favorite park, stopped the car, we got out and then he got down on one knee, pulled a ring box out of his pocket, opened it, showed it to me and formally asked me to marry him. Of course, I said yes and then he gently slid the ring on my finger.

Sometimes it is hard to put into words how you feel because the emotion is so overpowering and that was exactly how I felt at that exact moment, completely overwhelmed with love for Frank.

6

rabbit hunting

Time was moving very fast for us now and we had so much to do before Frank would leave for Army Basic Training. We only had eleven more days to spend together before Frank would leave.

I knew some of Frank's family from the church but others who lived in nearby towns wanted to meet me and were inviting us to their homes for supper.

An aunt and uncle of Frank's who lived in Sweeny, Texas were the first to invite us to supper. Frank and I had a great time at his uncle and aunt's home in Sweeny and after it got dark we left their home then headed back to Van Vleck.

Frank and I drove out of Sweeny then he turned left off of highway 35 onto the Pledger highway and then turned right onto Old Van Vleck road. We were listening to the radio driving along when Frank asked me a question.

"Nancy have you ever been rabbit hunting?"

Wondering what he was up to now because of memories of our "star gazing," I replied, "No, Frank, I have never been rabbit hunting."

We had not gone very far when Frank pulled the car over and stopped. Frank opened his car door, got out of the car, shut the door then since the driver's side window was rolled down said to me through the driver's window, "Slide over Nancy, you are going to be the driver."

Laughing, I did as he told me then Frank said, "Nancy, you will need to slowly pump the brakes when I tap on the windshield while I sit on the hood. The brakes have a little problem. Also, Nancy Lou, you will be driving without the car headlights on."

Shaking my head, I told him, "Really, Frank? Are you kidding me?"

Laughing and ignoring my question, Frank walked back to the trunk of his car, opened the trunk, got his gun, and a spotlight out of the trunk then he shut the trunk. Frank walked back up to the car on the passenger side, reached in the rolled down the window of the passenger door while holding the cord to the spotlight in his hand, unplugged the cigarette lighter, and then plugged the spotlight into the cigarette lighter hole.

Frank placed the gun on the hood of the car and with the spotlight in his hand; he climbed up on to the hood of the car, leaned back against the windshield, turned on the spotlight then placed his gun across his lap. Frank tapped on the windshield to get my attention and to let me know to put the car in drive and start moving.

Without the headlights on, I was straining to see the road and trying to keep the car on the road, when suddenly Frank tapped on the windshield. I pushed the brake quickly to the floorboard but the car did not stop, so I quickly stomped the brake again which made the car come to an abrupt stop. Frank went quickly sliding off of the hood of the car then the car rolled a little forward.

I was terrified and horrified at the same time! Did I just kill him? Suddenly a bright light shone through the driver's window and into my face and it was the game warden.

As I looked into the light I kept saying over and over, "I killed him! I killed him! I killed him!"

I looked towards the hood, pointing, when a hand reached up on to the hood of the car and Frank pulled himself up from the ground. I was thanking God Frank was alive!

The Game Warden asked Frank, "Son, have you been shooting from the road?"

Frank looked at me and then looked at the game warden then said, "No, sir, I didn't get a chance to."

The game warden asked Frank if he was all right and Frank told him he was. The game warden did not give us a ticket but as he was leaving, he turned back and told Frank, "Son, you might want to get a better driver!"

The game warden laughed all the way back to his car which was backed into a side road we had passed. The game warden had evidently seen the whole ordeal.

On February 24, 1968, Frank and I attended the Sweetheart Dance at the High School Cafeteria. We danced and enjoyed talking to our friends but afterward went to a quiet place to be alone to talk. This would be our last night together before Frank left the next day for basic training.

We talked until the wee hours of the morning and I got home way past my curfew but neither one of us cared. We were fixing to spend ten weeks apart which was nearly more time than we had been a couple and we were both totally overwhelmed by the fact that we would be separated from each other.

The next day Frank, his parents, brother, sister, my parents, brothers, and friends went to the airport to see Frank and Jimmy off. We watched them board the plane and take off.

Tears rolled down my face as the plane flew off but I also knew that I was strong enough to handle the ten weeks ahead and Frank was too!

7

leaving on a jet plane

Frank had boarded an airplane at Hobby Airport in Houston, Texas, on the afternoon of February 25, 1968, and my brother, Jimmy, was with him. The airplane was headed for Fort Leonard Wood, Missouri where they would do their Army Basic Training.

Frank wrote his first letter to me aboard that airplane. He was worried, nervous, and a little scared of what was to come at Fort Leonard Wood.

> *February 25, 1968*
> *Dear Nancy,*
> *This letter is coming to you from 33,000 feet in the air. I'm writing this at 6:15 P.M. from this sickening thing they call a jet. Let me tell you, it was and still is hell on this damn contraption. I am sorry if you felt I was acting funny, I probably was knowing me. I apologize for my actions. I have never been sadder in all my life than when we had to say goodbye this afternoon. I have already started counting the minutes and seconds until my 9 weeks are up and we will be married. We've had 3 of the most wonderful weeks that I have ever known and I want you to know that these past 3 weeks were only a few that we will spend together.*
> *Nancy, I want to thank you for being you, for being the most wonderful girl I have ever met. I'll let you know where to write me as soon as I find out where you can send me those letters you promised. I apologize for writing in pencil but it is all I had. Just remember the things I told you and remember you're my girl and I love you very much. I'm already missing you. Just remember me in your prayers and think about me every now and then.*
> *All my love, Frank.*

P.S. Come on and smile!!! If I sound goofed up, it's because I am.

There was absolutely no doubt that Frank was feeling lots of emotions in the above letter but when I read it I knew he was strong and he would face whatever difficulties that were to come.

When Frank and Jimmy left on the airplane in Houston, Texas, it was warm. They were wearing short-sleeved dress shirts and slacks. They were in for a surprise! Frank's next letter tells about that surprise.

> *February 27, 1968*
> *Dear Nancy,*
>
> *It's now 0733 (7:33 a.m.) and I'm lying in my bunk half asleep writing this letter to you. We got to St. Louis 7:30 p.m. and took a bus to Leonard Wood at 2200 (10:00 p.m.). We got at Leonard Wood (Hell!!) 1:00 a.m. and took a bus from there to the base at 1:30 a.m. When we got to the (censored) base we were taken by a taxi to the reception center. At this time, it was misting rain and 30°. From 2:00 a.m. Tuesday morning, when we got here, until 9:00 a.m. Tuesday morning, we were told what to do, where to do it and why in the hell it was that way.*
>
> *The picture enclosed could get me 6 months in the stockade. But instead of turning it in like I was supposed to, I hid it when they checked my wallet and saved it. DO NOT, I repeat DO NOT THROW IT AWAY, I want it!!! I had my 1st cigarette at 12:00 p.m. Tuesday, we were allowed to smoke only in the latrine (bathroom). It was about 38° today and it was cold and it was cold standing in lines and being cussed and chewed out for doing nothing but putting your hands in your pockets to*

keep warm. Jim and I were cussed and made run all the way back to the barracks while they (2 Sergeants) threw rocks at us for stepping on a blade of grass.

Everybody is on our ass and we have to do things like stand out in the cold for hours until they decide what they want to do with us. We took a shower and shaved a while ago, it was nice except there is no hot water, it is all ice cold. Well, I have to close and get some sleep. I haven't had any yet except the ½ hour I got Sunday night. I want you to know that this place is pure hell and I hate every S.O.B Sergeant in the whole damn Army. As soon as I get my address, I'll let you know and you better send me a letter quickly thereafter. Nancy, I miss you so much I want to cry. I miss seeing you because I have no picture to look at, only memory. Be sweet and take care of yourself because I love you and hope everything is alright.

All my love, Frank

P.S. How's the wedding planning going? Say hi to your folks and Mark and David for me

Frank's first week at basic training was really hard on him and his buddies. He had to send my picture home to me in his first letter and he was not getting any mail from me because I did not have his address. All I could do was read his letters, worry and cry in my bed at night. I was going to school and trying to plan our wedding but I really just wanted to be with him.

8

lonely in a crowd

The next letters Frank wrote was after he had been in basic training for one week. I was so excited when the next two letters arrived.

March 3, 1968
Dear Nancy,
Last night had to be the loneliest night of my life. It was Saturday night and everyone was sad because they were all thinking about how it was last Saturday night and they were all wishing they were home. Darling, I missed you so much I almost died.

I met some nice guys who have become some real buddies. This one who sleeps next to mine and Jimmy's bunk has been going with his girl for three years and we spent all night walking fire watch around the barracks. We were authorized to question anybody and see their papers and if they didn't show them we were to take them down to the Orderly's room. I went upstairs and when I came back my friend had checked downstairs and there were two guys in the latrine, so I started cussing them and giving them hell and they started getting smart, so I told them I was going to take them to the Orderly room, well I started for them and they showed me their papers and come to find out I had been cussing 2 Sergeants!

We ship out tomorrow and by next weekend we ought to have a permanent address and the next letter you get I should have a permanent so, I expect a letter soon afterward, that is if you want to. Don't get mad if I don't write you every day, I'll write you whenever I get a chance. I love to write you and I'll be so happy when I get your first letter but Honey I have to pull duties and scrub the barracks and all sorts of things. Nancy don't write me if you don't want to. I want to see you very much and hear from you very much. I hope you still love me as much as you did when I left. I love you as much or even more. We all lay around and think at night. We hate the night because everything gets quiet and all you can do is think about your girl and home. Nancy, I've never missed anyone the way I miss you, all I do is lay on my bunk and get a picture of your face in my mind and just look at you and see how pretty you are. You won't believe this but this is the 1st time I've ever written a sentimental letter. I never wrote one to anyone else because I never felt this way over any other girl. Behave and keep that chin up and most of all, be happy and think about me and how much I miss you.

Just remember, Nancy, I love you very much and I want very much to make you my wife in 9 weeks.

All my love,

Frank

P.S. How's our wedding plans coming along? Go out and see Momma and Daddy every now and then, they would like that.

Frank did not know that I was writing him letters but without an address, I could not send him my letters. He had only been gone a week but we had been seeing each other every day and now we were apart. Frank knew how much I loved him but he was lonely and tired. He did not know that I was missing him just as much as he missed me.

In the following letter, Frank sent me his address and asked me several questions he would like answered by me.

March 5, 1968

Dear Nancy,

Well, we arrived at Basic yesterday, (Monday) and I got put on Detail last night from 1900 (7:00 p.m.)

and got back at 2050 (8:50 p.m.) and lights went out at 2100 (9:00 p.m.). Today we started exercises and it was hell. I got my address and I expect some letters quickly. It is:

Pvt. Loren F. Henderson Sr.

RA (Not typing it)

Co. B-1-3

Ft. Leonard Wood, Mo. 65473

When you write to me do exactly like that.

I would have written to you yesterday night but I had no time because of the details! In 9 weeks from today, I'll be through with Basic. I thought as you thought that it would be only 8 weeks but we spent 1 week at the reception station and we will spend 1 week here before we start basic training. I'm sorry Honey but I can't help it, I am as disappointed as you. I'm sick and tired of this damn place and I wish I was home with you right now. I'm going mad waiting for you and dreaming of you (not bad dreams either). I miss you so much I don't know what to do.

Baby, there are a few things I want from you in your first letter.

(1.) How long it takes for my letter there?

(2.) If you love me as much as before?

(3.) If you still Love me enough to marry me?

(4.) If the other two answers are yes, fill me in on all the plans.

Don't get mad but those questions have been bothering me the most. Well, I'll have to close because I have to s, s, and s (shave, shit, and shower) before I go to bed and I have to mop and polish the floor. I'm getting pretty depressed so don't let my letters get you down or don't think I don't love you or don't think about you a lot.

Be good and remember I love you.
All my Love,
Frank
P.S. I think for my school, I'll be stationed in Vir-
ginia or Georgia. I signed up for single rotary turbine
helicopter maintenance.
Tell your Ma, Pa, Grady, Mark, and David hi for
me ok?
I MISS YOU!

I was missing Frank so much and I knew he was not receiving mail from me causing him to have so many doubts. Now, that I had his address and I would mail my letters with my undying love for him but it would take days for those letters to arrive.

As I have said before, we did not have email or Skype in the sixties. We only had landline telephones and letters which, once mailed, would take days to be received.

The wedding plans for Frank and I were in steady motion but I was having a hard time concentrating on the plans and missing him there by my side. I was so worried about him. I wanted him home so I could just hold him and tell him how much I loved him.

9

please, mr. postman

The next letter from Frank shows just how upset and isolated he was feeling. He had not received my letters but they were at least on the way.

March 7, 1968,
Dear Nancy,
I finally got a pen (19 cents). I wanted to write you this letter in ink for a change. As you know, I'm lonely after a week and I'm tired both physically and mentally and Nancy, like I warned you before I left, I'm liable to say anything when I get in my depressed moods so don't think anything about it because you know I love you and trust you.

I guess you are getting tired of hearing the same old, I miss you, I love you and write me but that is exactly the way I feel. I listen to mail call every day for my name and get disappointed if you don't but I understand, I guess you are busy. After I wrote you last night, I was so nervous that I was shaving and somebody yelled and I jumped and ripped my chin wide open for about 3 inches. I was supposed to go get stitches but I was too busy and If I missed anything, I would have to make it up and be late getting out.

Please send me your picture as soon as you get one. Well, I have to clean the latrine at 8:30 p.m. and it is fifteen after and then at 4:00 a.m.-5:00 a.m. I have to stand fire watch. Baby, I can't tell you how I feel. I can try but I know I can't get it across, so just believe me when I tell you, I love you very much and miss you tremendously.

All my Love,
Frank

P.S. Have you been out to see Mama (Mother-in-law) and Daddy (Father-in-law)?

I remember getting the above letter from Frank and it really upset me. Frank was always smiling and very calm in all situations but he was really feeling the intensity of basic training. My heart hurt for Frank but I knew there was nothing I could do which made me cry and feel worthless at the time. I prayed that he would receive my letters quickly because I had sent them by airmail.

Frank kept on writing to me knowing in his heart how much I loved him and that soon he would get letters from me.

March 10, 1968
Dear Nancy,

How are you doing kid? Let me tell you something, I love you very much. Hey, they just started playing, "I Love You", it fits, doesn't it.

Let me tell you what happened a few days before we got here, one guy hung himself, one guy got cut on the back 10 times with a razor and one got his head pushed out a 2nd story window. Everyone has crutches or is limping or has been to sick call. But I am ok and I'll make it. We get our guns tomorrow and Sunday I plan to go to church (I did last Sunday, too). I'm still waiting on those letters and a picture. I can't tell you how it is up here. (I'll try ... Hell.)

I am known as Tex and everyone wants to know if we still kill Indians and wear ten-gallon hats and boots. We finally got to go to the PX tonight and get a few items like a sewing kit, etc. Nancy, I'll have to finish this letter tomorrow because I have CQ watch tonight in 10 minutes and I have to take a shower and shave and make up my bed.

Well, I'm back (3:07 p.m.) the next day. We got the afternoon off (WOW) after we took our pictures in our class a uniform for our Co. B book. Look, kid, I took out some saving bonds in your name. At $6.25 a month, we will get 1 every 3 months ($18.75). I named Miss Nancy L. Blakley as the beneficiary because soon Miss Nancy L. Henderson will be Mrs. Loren F. Henderson, Jr. I'm getting over being depressed all the time and learning to laugh again. I still miss you but I'm learning to take it better (except on nights, especially tonight which is Saturday). I'm going to church tomorrow like I did last Sunday.

Well, write me if you get a chance, I'll be more than glad to hear from you.

Talk is that we get out May 2, but don't bank on it.

54 more days to go

Frank

P.S. Don't forget, I love the hell out of you. Be good and please write me and let me know how the Wedding is coming along.

Frank had left on February 27, 1968, for Fort Leonard Wood, Missouri but spent a week at the reception area and then went to the basic training where he finally received an address where I could send him letters. Rereading his letters truly makes my heart hurt now. Mail service was so slow back in 1968.

10

marching in the snow

Frank had been gone for over two weeks when I got the next letter from him. Just when he was beginning to adjust to being away from home, Mother Nature gave him a new form of adjustment.

March 13, 1968
Dear Nancy,

Last night (Monday), it started snowing, well it started snowing while we were in the theater listening to some men talk, and it snowed all night and all day today until about 5:00 this afternoon and it was so damn cold. We had to march about 1 mile to the theater and 1 mile back two times today and the snow was about 6 to 8 inches deep and then the sun came out and it started to melt and it was slick as hell. We had to wear liners in our field jackets, two pairs of pants and a pair of overshoes. Have you ever tried to run in the snow? It's hell.

Right now, we are going to classes and seeing films on malaria, airborne and lots of stuff. We got our rifles yesterday. I didn't get your letter today but I understand, I guess you are pretty busy. You ought to send me a list of songs because right now I can't think of anything but how much I love you and how much I miss you. Your letters are about all that keeps me going. They can do anything to me they want but keep me from mail call at 4:30. I thank God every night for you and your love because I feel I'm very fortunate to have you. You know what my parents said about you? They said the loved you and that they felt I was very lucky to have someone like you. I feel I'm very fortunate too.

My good buddy and his wife are going to come down from Iowa for my wedding I think. I like that blue (turquoise) for our Bridesmaids, it looks good. Everyone in my barracks likes it too. I have to serve at chow in the morning at 5:00 a.m., clean the latrine, s-s-s and fold up my washed clothes tonight, so I'd better go. Remember, I love you more than anything in the world.

All my love always,

Frank (7 weeks and 5 days)

P.S. Be good and remember I love you very much and write me as much as you can and keep on loving me.

I LOVE YOU, LOU!

I was so happy to see that Frank had regained his beautiful spirit. Just that he called me Lou was a sign that he was in a more care-free relaxed spirit. Lou was his pet name for me and I loved it. I don't recall anyone ever calling me Lou before Frank did.

March 14, 1968

Dear Nancy,

Today, we had a fun day (whoopee), we did our exercises in the snow (you know that white stuff) push-ups and all. I'm so tired I'm about ready to drop. We had two guys carried to the hospital today with something. I sleep next to one and the other one sleeps not 10 feet from me. I hope it's not that spinal meningitis or what the hell.

I feel rejected because I haven't got any mail in 2 days, (I'm just kidding really).

I'm doing alright, I'm kind of tired but I'm feeling great. Just think 7 weeks and 3 days and you'll be Mrs. L. F. Henderson, Jr., (If you still want to). The snow is melting and it's getting messy.

Write me and send me a good picture of you so I can show everyone my future wife. Nancy, I'm so tired I can't think of anything to say except that you are constantly on

*my mind and in my prayers. So be good and remember I
love you so very much.*
Your lonely soldier who loves you very much,
Frank
P.S. Goodnight

It was so good to be able to write to Frank and receive
letters back with answers to my questions.

It was hard to only have letters as a way of communication
but there is also such a rare beauty to handwritten letters. You
can actually see how a person is feeling by their writing. Seems
as though the emotions people are having as they hand write
a letter magically come out as their hand holds the pen as it
magically flows across the page.

I could tell by Frank's writing if he was tired, sad, depressed,
happy, scared, excited or worried. When Frank would write
down that he loved me, I could see as I read his love for me not
only in the words he had written but in the way his pen had
beautifully written the words.

Frank would write to me as if he was actually talking to me
while I was sitting in a chair in the room next to him, instead
of hundreds of miles away. He wanted me to see through his
words what he was seeing, doing and experiencing, so I could
be a real part of his soul and heart. We were totally open and
honest with each other from the moment we both knew we
were in love.

11

basic training fun

I sent Frank my senior picture in a letter right before receiving the following two letters from him. I still had my braces on but that did not keep me from smiling for the picture, just for him.

> *March 16, 1968*
> *Dear Nancy,*
> *This letter is going to be dedicated to answering your questions in the latest letters today, Saturday, March 16, 1968, but first I have to tell I love you very much and that's 3 small words to cover a very strong undefinable feeling I have for you.*
>
> *You asked about the exercises. Yes, they are hard but I'm getting in better condition and it's getting easier. To pass and graduate you need 300 pts. There are 5 fields and each field are worth 100 pts. (if you get a perfect score). The fields are the rifle (if you hit 60 out of 87 you get an expert and 100 pts.), the mile run (6 minutes and 10 seconds for 100 pts.), a crawl on your stomach for 20 yds. down and 20 back in 32 seconds, the bars (74 in 2 minutes and (?) seconds for 100 pts.) and you have to carry someone 150 yds. on your back of your own weight, ½ way and they carry you back the other half in 36 seconds for a 100 pts. To get a pass or PX privileges we have to answer 168 military questions out of 168. The letters you write I can keep as long as I have room, I'm keeping them right now in my empty shaving kit.*
>
> *I'm getting a letter every other day but don't think I'm mad at you because you can't help it if the mail service is slow, so don't worry about it because I'm not. I know you love me and will write me when you can and it will get here when it does. And damn it I'll love you whether you have braces on or not. I love you as a person,*

not as a mouth, eye, nose or ears. Hey, I can't wait to see your hair, from the way you talk it's getting pretty and long. Don't go to any bother I mean if you would rather it be short and if it's easier to keep that way then get it cut. I'll like it any way you wear it. If I ever hear you say please don't stop loving me or I'll die again I'll personally kick your butt. You know that it is impossible for me to stop loving you. So, knock it off because I don't want you to doubt me because it's there and it always will be for you. Don't worry about me so much I'm alright, I'll make it. Remember, I went to school at VVHS and we were tough, (HA, HA). Perk up yourself and get off this nervous breakdown crap because the days will pass (24 hrs. Every day) and eventually I'll be there and I'll be the same old guy that left. Except, I'll be getting married in a few days.

If you don't straighten up and be happy and take care of yourself, I'll divorce you. No, seriously, it's important to be happy because the time will pass faster and easier if you face it with a smile and forget about feeling sorry for yourself. You ought to be happy because I love you and am looking forward to that wonderful day. Hey, by the way, we had a formal Inspection today and we had to put on our dress uniform and my zipper broke on mine all the way down and I was in bad shape when the Captain came in but he didn't spot it. Lou, if I told you what my parents have said about you, you'd be so happy. They told me they loved you very much and they like you more every time they see you. Every letter is about you and what you've said and everything. I'm learning to laugh too. Everybody's getting to know each other better and joke.

Right now, Jim came down (He's in the 1st. Platoon down the hall, I'm in the second) and all my men in my barracks are playing cards. The second Platoon (which is the one I'm in) got the best barracks of the week today after Inspection and this made me pretty proud because we worked until 9:10 last night getting everything ready until 10:00 this morning. I plan to go to church tomorrow, Jim and I for the 3rd week straight, (pretty good huh). Well, I bet you are surprised at the length of this letter, well so am I, but I felt like writing and I'm feeling good because all I can think of is how happy I'll be. I'll have to close now but keep writing and let me know things.

Remember I'm crazy over you and I love you very much. I know we are far apart but it's not the end of the world. So, chin up and be and be happy. Ok. All My Love

Frank

P.S. I LOVE YOU VERY MUCH

P.S.P.S. Tell Mom to keep writing me and Dad and Lloyd. Be good Darling and think of me and most important be happy.

Frank and I were really beginning to feel the strain of being apart but we were writing to each other trying to perk each other up. Frank was getting used to his physical training and making new friends in the barracks which was helping him get through his loneliness.

I was planning our wedding with my mom and Frank's mom but wanting Frank to be by my side to discuss the plans with him although I knew he would be happy with the decisions that were made. Actually, I let my mom and Frank's mom make most of the decisions because they were having so much fun planning our wedding.

I was going to school Monday through Friday which kept me busy on those days. It was the last few months of my Senior year and there was so much to do but the weekday evenings were lonely but as Frank has said the weekends were truly very long and lonely. Frank and I had spent every waking moment of every weekend together before he left.

> *March 20, 1968*
> *Dearest Darling,*
> *How's that for an opening? I thought it was pretty good for me!*
> *Well, we had our pt. today (Tuesday) instead of Friday. Boy, am I tired. First, we had the 40yd. low crawl through sand and the minimum time for 100pts. was 22 seconds, I made it in 41 seconds which was fair and worth 49pts. Jim got 54pts. Then we had to go to the bars, maximum of 76 in one minute. I made 60 and fell off. I got 80pts and Jim got 57 bars. Next, we had the dodge, jump and run, maximum 22 seconds. I made it in 22.5 and got 95pts. Jim did 23.5 and got 80 something points. Next was the 150yard man carry, where you had to carry a man of your own weight 150 yards, maximum of 41 seconds. I made it in 43 seconds for 95 points. Jim made it in 46 seconds. Next was the bad ass, the mile-run. I felt like shit running because my chest is full of shit and when I cough I cough up a little blood and snot and all kind of shit so I had trouble breathing, maximum time 8 minutes 30 seconds. I made it in close to 7 minutes and Jim made it in 7 minutes. Anyway, when I was running and hurt so bad, I thought of you and it made the road a lot easier to go and a lot more pleasant.*

Well to qualify, you had to have 300 points and I wound up with about 408 points out of 500 points, so I didn't do so bad. I think Jim might have made 400 points, I don't know. But I got a letter from my old man today and I read it and now I'm writing you. I know I'll get some mail from you tomorrow, I hope.

Well, may I ask you a question?

When you write me let me know what letters you have gotten, so I'll know how caught up on matters you are. Hey, I love you. Hey, beautiful get your damn head up and smile. We are allowed to have one picture in a frame in our locker, so when you get a recent picture of yourself with your braces off, send it so I can see what you look like with the barbed wire off (HA! HA!) If you look anything like you do with them on you'll be simply beautiful.

Darling, I miss you and love you so very much.

I'm keeping my chin up and trying to be pleasant as I can because like I said it'll make things easier to take. I hope you are taking care of yourself and being good because if you're running around barefoot I'll kick your butt personally.

Well, baby, I'm going to have to close because I have to polish my boots and mop the floor and s, s, s and study my test booklet because I have a test coming up. So, remember I love you and need you very, very much (wow, two very). Take care and keep loving me. Ok? OK.

All my love forever,

Frank

P.S. I love the hell out of you. I wish I could explain just how much I love you but all I can come up with is I love you more than anything else in this whole world.

Rumor has it we get out May 3rd. I love you so damn much it's pitiful.

> *Love Me?*
> *I LOVE YOU*

Even though Frank was doing well in his physical training, he was also very sick. He was afraid to go to the infirmary because he thought it would set him back and keep him from completing basic training with his buddies. He was also worried he would not make it home on time for our wedding which was planned for May 8th.

Frank's last letter had me so worried about him. He was trying to make light of being sick but I knew he was just trying to keep me from worrying.

12

young love

Frank's next letter really upset me. Frank was so far from home and so sick. As soon as Frank could, he would call home to his folk's house collect from a phone booth, so I could talk to him.

> *March 25, 1968*
> *Dear Nancy,*
> *This a very depressing letter, so if you want to throw it away do it now. Thursday night I got two shots and then at 6:00-8: 30 p.m., I had to clean the Mess Hall and then at 3:30 a.m. Friday morning until 9:00p.m. Friday night (18 and 1/2 hrs.) I had K.P. Saturday, we had an inspection and our platoon won the best of the week (yea). Then we had a test, the cut off was 140 out of 168 questions. I made 151 and didn't even study. Well, after the test I felt cold and we had PX privileges yesterday afternoon.*
> *But Friday night, I left my pants on my footlocker and the next day I checked and someone had stolen every penny I had about ten bucks. So, I didn't go to the PX and drink beer with everyone else. Everyone else tried to give me money, but I was feeling poorly and I didn't go. Well, at supper I ate a ½ bowl of soup and a piece of cherry pie.*
> *Well, this morning I felt like shit and had a fever and chills. So, I skipped breakfast and slept and missed church. At dinner, I had to serve and I ate one small ham sandwich and skipped supper. To sum it up, I ache all over, have a fever, I'm sweating and have chills also. Jim bought me some 4-way cold tablets and I took two and they gave me stomach cramps. The guy that sleeps across from me has had URI (Upper Respiratory Infection)*

and he says that is what I have. I don't know. But, I'm not going to the hospital because I'll miss some training.

But don't worry because I'll get better, I promise. Everyone is taking care of me and I'll get better. I shouldn't have told you but if you had found out later you would probably get mad. If Mom and them ask, tell them all I'm ok. I'm sorry my writing is slow but I haven't had time. I write every chance I get. By the way, don't send any more letters airmail because it took three days to get here, so don't waste your money.

I've gotten two letters this week from you and one from my family. The mail must be screwed up. I ordered two 8 x 10 pictures of me in my uniform. One for you and one for my family. About the BC pills do what your mother said and after we get married you can stop but please her for now.

Well, how's everything going with you? I believe I've cried on your shoulder for long enough. I feel bad for pushing all my troubles on you, so forget I ever said anything. I love you so very, very much. I took your picture out a while ago and just stared at you. I love you and miss you so very much.

Do you miss me? Darling, I love you.

Don't you or my parents send me any money because I can make it until payday (Friday)? Keep your chin up and don't worry about me because BT is getting easier and the time is passing. I'm not as bad off as you think, I just don't feel real, good, it's probably the food so, don't worry.

Ok. Lou, I can't tell you how much I love you. Well, be good and tell my parents I'm writing as much as I can and not to worry about me. Nancy, remember one

thing, I love you so very much. See you later Mrs. Loren F. Henderson, Jr. (future).
      Love,
      Frank

Frank was really sick and I was extremely worried about him. Of course, I let his folks know that he was sick. I knew how worried they were about him and his welfare.

This letter of all the letters is one you should remember as you read this book. It will play an important part in the far future.

> *April 8, 1968*
> *Dear Lou,*
>   *God Damn, I miss you so much! Baby today I got to hear your wonderful voice and talk to you, you, beautiful woman. Baby, I finished talking to you at 2:30 and we caught a cab back to the barracks and tried to take a test. The radio was going and playing songs we used to listen to and it blew my mind and I made 156 instead of 165, so I don't get a pass or post privileges next week. But I don't care because I got to talk to my beautiful, wonderful fiancée.*
>   *Baby, I love you so much, It's getting where I can't stand being away from you anymore. The only thing that keeps me going is that may be on at night I'll get a letter from you and boy do I enjoy that. If you knew how much I love you, you wouldn't ask "I hope you love me still" or some silly shit like that. Baby, I do love you and I always will. You're my everything and I don't think I would want to live without you and I don't plan on trying. Baby, you're on my mind constantly.*

I 'll be so damn glad when I get home to you and can hold you in my arms and tell you exactly how I feel about you.

Girl, you couldn't find a better husband you tried. I will treat you so good and provide for you as well as I can. I just can't tell you how much I miss you. Girl, I enjoyed talking to you so much today. Hell! Guess what just came on the radio? You guessed it, "Young Girl".

Baby, I'll have to close now because it's almost lights out, so I'll write anytime I can and keep writing me as often as you can. Remember, first of all, I love you with all my heart, soul, and mind.

Love,

Frank

P.S. You should have seen me strutting around with your picture today showing everyone.

Hi Wife!!!

Frank got to call me and it was absolutely wonderful. I remember how excited I was to hear his voice again. I was on cloud nine and floating on cloud nine, just as he was. Our love was so deep for each other. We had been separated from each other for weeks but our love had only become stronger and deeper. God had put us together and there was no doubt that we were becoming one heart, soul, and mind with God's blessings.

13

why does a man cuss?

I wrote a letter to Frank about the increase in cuss words in his letters to me. The following letter is his explanation for why a man cusses.

April 9, 1968
Dear Nancy,
Girl, I am severely disappointed in you. I got three letters from you today and the 3rd one, (April 6), made me feel very bad. You know I love you very much and for me to love someone commands a great deal of respect for that person. I respect you more than I have respected anyone in my entire life. I asked you to marry me and be my wife.

Nancy marriage to me is one of the most important and wonderful things that can happen to a man and I'm the type that wouldn't make the decision of getting married to someone I didn't respect.

I cuss in my letters to you because up here everyone cusses all the time and cussing for us is a way to relieve inner tensions. I'm sorry if you feel that my cussing is being disrespectful to you because that is entirely wrong and you should know it by now. I cuss because that is something a man does to relieve the feelings inside. If I get mad I cuss, if I'm happy I cuss, and if I'm trying to express myself or describe something, I cuss. It's just natural for me. I hate that you think that I have no respect for you because I do and if my cussing makes you think that then I'll quit when I'm around you.

I'll do anything you ask to show that I love you and respect you to the utmost. If you only knew how much I really love you, miss you, and respect you, you would know better than to think that. You said that you have gained respect for yourself. You've learned all the things I told you, you would about yourself.

Girl, just remember one thing, I love you and respect you very much and I always will. This letter is not to fuss you out or anything but I just wanted to explain how I felt and try to answer your question and ease your mind. Nancy, my heart aches at night for you. I miss you terribly and I'll be so glad when I get to be with you again. (Same old thing). I know in every letter I say about the same thing, that I'll be glad when you and I'll be together again but that is utmost in my mind.

I got Mama's brownies yesterday (Monday) and three letters from you postmarked 4, 5, 6, now do you believe that the mail is screwed up? I'm writing this from the CQ desk, where I have duty at 3-4 in the morning and it's 5 to 4 now and we get up 4:25, so as soon as my relief comes down I'll have to cut it off and try to catch 25 more minutes of sleep.

He is here now so goodbye for now.

All My Love,

Frank

P.S. I think you are the most beautiful and nice girl I have ever known and I'm very proud to call you my fiancée' and future wife.

Well, from the response I got from Frank, it seems that I was a little rough on him in my letter from the 6th of April 1968. Frank had never cussed around me or in spoken words to me, so I was a little shocked as his letters kept increasing with more and more cuss words which made me wonder how much he respected me.

After I wrote to Frank about the cussing, he never wrote another cuss word in a letter to me but just to let me know that he was deliberately leaving the cuss words out of his letters just for me, he would substitute the appropriate number of dashes, one to represent each letter in the cuss word, exactly one dash for each letter.

I love how he loved me, I loved how he would do anything for me, and I knew that I would always have to be very careful to not change him too much but to change myself to accept him just the beautiful way he was because he was such a very special person.

The next letter spans over five days. I have dated it April 15, 1968, because that is the date it is postmarked.

> *April 15, 1968*
> *Dear Nancy,*
> *Darling, please believe me nothing the Army or anyone else could do to me could ever change the way I feel about you. Now quit feeling sorry for yourself and pick your head up like my future wife and fly right. I love you very much and I always will. All my life I've waited for someone who loved me and that I loved with all my heart and I finally found her.*
> *So, baby you know I love you with all my heart, so please believe in me, please. I can't look you in the eyes and tell you, so believe me when I tell you I love you. I'll finish this letter tomorrow or later because I have to go to bed and we have guard duty for 24 hours tomorrow.*
> *Well, we had guard duty last night and it was rough. We had to travel in twos with fixed bayonets because the guards had been getting jumped and robbed. But nothing happened.*
> *Here I am sitting on my _ _ _ _ and it's 15 to seven and we have shots at 7:25 p.m. and an inspection in class A's tomorrow at 8:00 a.m. We packed all of our gear this*

afternoon and Monday morning at 4:00 a.m. we leave for bivouac.

Wednesday we went to record range to qualify with the M14 rifle. If you hit 30 or under you be-lowed (didn't qualify), if you get 31 to 44 you won a marksman badge, 45 to 60 sharpshooter badge, 60 to 84 for an expert. You got 56 rounds and 56 targets on the first range and 40 rounds and targets on the second range. I was nervous and goofed up on the first range and got only 22 hits. So, on the next one, I had to relax, so I could qualify. So, I got 24 of 28 one of the best fired all day. So, I got 46 out of 84 and will get a sharpshooter badge or medal on graduation day. Jim also will get a sharpshooter.

I'm sitting here shooting the bull and all I can think of is I love you. Nancy, this is Sunday and I'm in no hurry or anything so I'll try to write where you can read it. I realize the parts written Wed. And Fri., are hard to read but I wanted to get a few lines off with the thought of finishing it but as usual, I didn't have time.

Lou, yesterday I guess was the loneliest day in my entire life, It was Saturday and only 35% of the men were supposed to get leaves that meant three out of each squad (13 men), so I told our Sergeant I didn't want one so a couple of my buddies who live in St. Louis and Chicago could go home. Well, there are about 6 of us left in my platoon and about 10 on our floor. Everyone was talking about going home and all so they all thanked me and said they really hoped I got a leave after Basic so I could get married.

So, Jim, Steve and I and a couple of other guys went to the EM Club and then came back. All we heard on the jukebox were songs that made me feel that much lonelier. Songs like "A Coming Home Soldier", "Soul and Inspi-

ration", "I'm Mr. Lonely", and many others that really got to me. We had one guy in our room who almost got bashed yesterday by me. He kept singing "Beautiful People" and that song really gets to me. Darling, I love you and miss you so much I can't think of anything but you.

Nancy, I want to clear one thing up now. You ask me if I will ever change my mind and you are afraid that I will. You said I probably felt the same way about you at one time, but you said you loved me and would never change your mind. I have never doubted you or even considered you changing your mind because I know you love me. I love you very much and will never change my mind or change the way I feel about you. Write and ask Jim what I'm always talking about. I eat, sleep, and talk Nancy. Girl, don't ever doubt my love for you again because it's there, believe me, it doesn't die, it just grows and grows. I don't know how but it does.

I've been thinking and May 11th sounds alright to me but don't plan on that day yet because I'm not sure but write me and give me your opinion on the day. The only reason on a thought of the 11th was that Crowley is in school and couldn't get off until the third weekend and Steve said he and his wife could make it by then also. The 11th is not definite because I still don't know how much or if I get any time after basics. My orders are in but I won't get them for ten more days. So let me know what you think about it because if you don't like it I'll think of something else.

Nancy, your letters are about all that keeps me going because I enjoy hearing from you so much. I know you probably like to hear from me every now and then also but I really try to write every chance I get, so don't get depressed if I don't get off more letters because I try to *honestly. Well, only three weeks to go and they are going to be ruff.*

We lost the Battalion Train fire Streamer by 7/10 of a point. Delta company won it and our SOI (Senior Drill Instructor) was mad. So we are working hard to win the PT Streamer. Lloyd knows how I feel about you, doesn't he? You had better straighten up or we'll have a hymn book session when I get home.

Don't ever stop loving me. Your love is the most cherished thing I possess. I will never do anything to damage the way you feel about me. I want to be with you forever and I'll do everything in my power to make you a good husband and make you happy at all times. You are the best thing that ever happened to me and I thank God every night for your love and for bringing me such a wonderful person as you.

ALL my Love for a Lifetime,

Frank

P.S. I have enclosed some pictures of myself. They are not good but what can you expect from a person like me anyway? Give my parents a few if you don't mind. Nancy, I love you more than I can ever tell you and the happiest day in my life will be the day you become my wife.

Frank was getting busier and I was too, but we were trying to communicate as much as possible. Frank still did not have his orders, so the wedding date was up in the air. Frank's Mom, my Mom and I were doing all we could do until we got a definite date from Frank on his graduation date and we still did not know if he would get leave to come home before his next assignment.

So many ifs but even more prayers were being said. I knew in my heart that I could not let Frank go off to his next assignment without becoming his wife first and I knew he felt the same way.

14

a unique and special letter

The next letter is unique and special. Frank decided to write to me on something he thought would be different, but I will let him tell you about it.

April 20, 1968
Dear Lou,
Isn't this a novelty?

I bet you never expected to get a letter that was written on a bedsheet. Well, I'm not out of paper, I'm not nuts, and I don't mean anything by it. I just thought that it would be unusual.

It is Friday of my 6th week and my nerves are shot. We don't get our orders until Wednesday and rumor is the RA's don't get a leave after basic. So, I'm about to go nuts. I got back from bivouac Thursday at 10:00. We ate chow and then we went and saw Bob Hope. It was great. He was really good.

Sweety, I'm tired tonight and I don't really feel like going into it but I'll tell you this much, it was hell. Excuse my language but it was exactly that and I know of no other way to define it. I'm not mad because you all decided on the 8th because anything you decide now is alright because you have about 2 weeks and the boss takes over.

Ha, Ha! Baby, your letters are putting me up in the sky, I love you and I need you so much, girl. When I get home, we're going to the beach and lay around all day. I should be polishing my muddy boots and getting things straightened up because we have inspection but I said, man what comes first Lou or the ____ Army.

All I can think of is songs like "Beautiful People", Johnny Rivers singing "Baby I Need Your Loving", and they just keep running through my weary mind. Today we went to the live grenade range to throw grenades and I enjoyed it. I'm so tired because we didn't get but from 2 to 4 hours sleep for a couple of nights. So, if I don't make much sense and cut this letter short, don't worry because I'm so darn tired.

Well, I just found out I have fire watch from 4 to 5 so there goes one more hour of sleep. Baby, I'm gonna have to close, but I've got so much to tell you, so if I talk your ears off when I get home don't think anything about it.

All My Love,

Frank

I Love You, Lou Only 1 week and 6 days to go

Frank was really tired and counting the days until basic training was over. I can read in his words how tired he is. He is rambling from one thing to the next as if his thoughts are circling in his mind. I knew Frank would make it but I was still worried about him because he was beginning to be nonchalant about what the Army wanted him to do but I knew that he was just very tired and would do his best when asked of him. Frank was not a slacker but a person who always gave at least 200% of himself in everything he did, he just needed some sleep.

April 22, 1968

Dear Lou,

How's everything going now Honey?

You'll never guess what time it is, 2:15 in the morning. I have CQ watch from 2-3. Well, yesterday was Saturday and instead of the usual Saturday morning inspection, we had bayonet training and a practice proficiency test. We finally got post privileges, not at noon but at 7:00 Saturday night. Well, baby guess what? You'll be living in Fort Devens, Massachusetts and be married to

a Radio Code man. We (ASA) received our assignments
Sat.

I still don't know if I'll be getting a leave or not. The
course will last for 13 weeks and it teaches the sending
and receiving of, Morse code. Following the 1st 13 weeks,
I'll be reassigned to a more specialized radio code school
which will vary from 9 to 15 weeks in length. Jim is
going to Virginia for his AIT and we both signed up for
the same thing, but neither one of us got our 5 choices.
He's signed up for power generator repair and air conditioning maintenance. Steve is assigned to the same thing
I am and is going to Devens also. I'm still sweating out
my orders to see if I get a leave. We should get them this
coming week.

Baby when I'm in our room I'm alright because all
the guys are laughing, joking, or talking but when I get
by myself, I have a hard time. All I can think of is you
and how much I miss you and need you. I may sound
silly but I hate the night because my mind is filled with
memories of us and this makes me sad because I'm not
there to hold you and be with you.

I think Mom is about as excited about the wedding
as I am and you are. She writes and fills me in on everything and even tries to draw me a picture of the bride's
bouquet. I can't wait to get married and set up house and
for you and I to live like a man and wife. The two of us
taking on the world and you know I believe we will win,
in fact I know we will because I'm not giving up, are you?
I bet you didn't even know I had left, did you.

I went to wake up Herman because he has the 3 to 4
CQ but I returned faithfully just like I will later (1 week
and 5 days). We take our first Pt test Wed and from 6 to
11:30 Friday night we have night infiltration where we

crawl under barbed wire and stuff under real machine fire. The machine gun will be fired over our backs as we crawl. So, I plan on keeping my butt down as low as possible or else I'll lose it.

Did I tell you Friday we had to throw a grenade? I enjoyed it. I was kind of nervous because if you let up on the handle 1/15 of an inch it will go off in 4 to 6 seconds. A sergeant just walked in drunker than a skunk.

Today we learned a little hand to hand combat (judo) and we will get more Monday and Tuesday.

How's school going? Getting all ready for graduation? Tell my brother that if he doesn't write pretty soon, I'm going to kick his --- when I get home.

Hey, Lou tell your parents to write Jim because he, just like me, likes to hear from home too. A guy up here can get all kinds of thoughts about home if people don't keep in touch. Hey in my room two guys went to the hospital with measles. Tell Mom, she is pretty smart making me get those measles shots. I'll be back in a minute, I think my buddy went back to sleep because it's 7 after 3 now so I better go see if he's getting up. I'm back (big deal) and he's coming so I'll finish up in the morning. Good night.

Well here I am on my bunk writing a conclusion on this letter which probably doesn't make any sense but I hope it does because all I wrote was true especially the part that says I love you. Baby, I love you so darn much I just can't start to stand to miss you. Does that make sense? We just got the message that North Koreans just attached U.S. forces in Korea, so it looks bad. I'm pretty shook up now because I feel a particular feeling for my country and its' way of life and I also feel for you because it wouldn't be right for you if I went, so I'm goofed up.

Don't worry about it I'll do enough worrying for myself and you.

Well, good night darling and remember me in your prayers. Be sweet and remember I love you very, very much.

All my Love,
Frank

Frank was definitely shaken by the news he had received about North Korea attacking U.S. forces. When he wrote me this letter his handwriting really showed his concerns. Frank had no idea if he would be sent to Korea or Vietnam after his graduation or if he would be coming home to me to get married. Everything was up in the air and very unsettling for him but I knew Frank would do whatever the Army asked of him and I knew I would stand by Frank in any way I possibly could whether married or not.

Frank had only one week and four days left in basic training. Would he get his leave to come home and marry me or go straight across the ocean to war? Those two questions kept running through my mind while I prayed and continued working on our wedding.

15

my brother's letter

There is a love that is often unspoken between best friends. Frank and Jimmy shared that unspoken love. Frank and Jimmy were best friends who had a deep love and respect for each other before Frank and I started dating. Frank and Jimmy had even joined the Army on the Buddy System, which meant they were to be stationed together throughout their service time in the Army and included them doing Basic Training together.

When Frank had gotten sick in Basic Training, Jimmy was the one who took care of him and bought Frank medicine. Frank always mentions Jimmy, as Jim, in most of his letters to let me know how my brother is doing on all of the physical training and tests.

Frank knew that I was concerned about my oldest brother who I was very close to, loved very much, and would want to know how he was doing.

I also wrote my brother, Jimmy, letters while he was in Basic Training. Checking on Frank while he was sick, letting him know I loved him and asking him questions about how he was doing.

I decided, after asking Jimmy for permission first, to include one of his letters home to me because he was such a part of Frank's and my life.

April 9, 1968
Dear Nancy,

I was just reading your letter. Well, don't be so shocked, I do write every once in a while and I was glad to hear from you As to your questions, the only one I can really answer is the Frank still cares for you very much and he cannot wait to get home to you.

The flu Frank got over with a few days ago. I have been getting a lot of mail from Linda and I hope to see her soon.

Nancy the Army is groovy and it is just what I needed to make me think. Time is running out for me. I really don't know where I go from here. I will probably to war and I will return but I may not.

So, let the kids and a few girls know, I need to be alone when I come home and that I miss them all.

Better close it is late. Write soon.

Your Bub

LOVE,

Jim

HA! HA! We will have Frank your Wedding Night!

While talking with my brother about his recall of Basic Training he told me that Frank and his first orders were to go to Vietnam and they were sent to train for that but then new orders came for them which would be the duty stations that Frank has mentioned in his letter written to me on April 22, 1968.

Frank would call me again on Saturday, April 27, 1968, and he was very excited. He told me that the rumor was they would graduate on Friday, May 3, 1968. Frank also told me with shouts of joy in that phone booth that he and Jimmy had been given leaves to come to Texas for two weeks before reporting to their next assignments.

I would not receive any more letters from Frank but he did call on Friday, May 3, 1968, after he graduated and told us that he and Jimmy would be flying home to Texas that night.

I was so excited and both of our families went to pick them up at Hobby Airport in Houston.

The letter above which written by my brother, Jimmy, really shows the emotions these young men felt. Jimmy would not go to Vietnam after basic training but in November of 1968, Jimmy would go to Vietnam only returning home for a thirty day leave in 1969 then back to Vietnam to return home in the middle of 1970. Jimmy volunteered to do "back to back" tours in Vietnam only broken by a few weeks home at to visit family.

As with all of these men who served their country in Vietnam, they were not welcomed home by a grateful nation but made to feel that their service was not appreciated which added to the PTSD that they would have from the horror of their experiences there. Of course, their families welcomed them home but there were not any parades of honor for them or open expressions of gratitude.

At a family reunion held at my home, my daughter-in-law's father, Jack Burt approached me after he had a conversation with my brother, Jimmy, and asked me if Jimmy had ever been "officially" welcomed home by a "grateful nation." Jack Burt is a member of the Matagorda County Calvary, an organization which welcomes home soldiers, escorts families of fallen soldiers, and so much more.

I told Jack that Jimmy had never been welcomed home by our nation, so he told me to give him ten minutes then he would do just that. After ten minutes passed then I asked everyone to go to my front yard. In less than a minute, Jack came rolling in on his motorcycle with music blaring, flags waving, and lights flashing. Jack got off of the motorcycle, went to Jimmy, shook Jimmy's hand, and "officially" welcomed Jimmy home from a belated "grateful nation"!

So many of the young people standing in my front yard had not been born when the Vietnam War happened and along with the older generation, they were all truly affected by Jack's beautiful "Welcome Home" for Jimmy. There was not a dry eye in the front yard.

Jimmy was shocked, honored, thankful, and very overwhelmed, as he hugged all there then thanked Jack Burt.

For all of those reading this post, if you served and were not welcomed home, "Welcome Home!" from us all.

The love between best friends, whether it be two men, two women, or a woman and a man, is really the most beautiful thing and should never be something that we are afraid to express.

Jimmy and Frank not only shared "Best Friend Love" but after Frank and I married they shared "Best Friend Brother Love" for one another.

Jimmy is the oldest of my siblings and has always taken care of our children, our grandchildren, and us all. He is the beautiful kind of God given man who would literally give you the shirt off of his back because he has so much love for others in his heart. Jimmy loves others the way God intended that we love each other.

Since Frank died, Jimmy has called me nearly every single day, checking on me, asking if I need anything, and telling me how much he loves me. I am so proud of my oldest brother and I love him with all of my heart.

Frank is looking down on his best friend and brother, smiling proudly at the friend and brother he loves so much. No doubt in my mind that God is, too.

16

stuck on you

Wow! I had Frank in my arms and it seemed that God had used super glue on our hands and we could not let go.

Things were really busy in Van Vleck, Texas. It seemed like everyone in this town were in some way involved in our wedding. Since the wedding was planned for the evening of May 8, 1968, at the First Methodist Church in Van Vleck, Texas there was so much to do but it was hard for Frank and me to concentrate on all of the "pomp and circumstance" when all we wanted to do was be alone with each other.

It seemed that we were lost in our own little world with each other while my mom and Frank's mom were running around getting everything together. Our mothers kept trying to get us on board with the wedding plans but we might have been too lost in each other but eventually gave in.

My folks' living room and dining room, which was a large room separated by two large brick planter boxes, one on either side of the room, had been converted into a wedding gift room. The dining room table was literally full of dishes, silverware, pots, pans, sheets, towels, blankets, knick-knacks, cooking utensils, toaster, electric skillets and just about everything a new couple would need to start out their new married life. While Frank was in basic training two wedding showers had been thrown for us which Frank's mom, my mom and I had attended.

Frank and I went through the all of these gifts together and we felt so blessed to have so many people that cared about us and had given us so many beautiful things. Frank and his family had lived in Matagorda County for many years, were well known, loved, and respected by many people. Even though my family had only lived in Van Vleck a short time, since my parents were both teachers, they were also known, loved, and respected by so many people.

Saturday, May 4, 1968, Frank and I had many things which include buying thank-you gifts for all who would be participating in our wedding.

Also, we got the required blood tests from a family doctor who opened his office up for us on a Saturday so we could go to the courthouse and get our marriage license on the following Monday.

Sunday, May 5, 1968, Frank and I attended church with our families then had lunch with one family and then dinner with the other.

Monday, May 6, 1968, was really hectic, we had so much to do but we were having so much fun together that the hours flew by quickly. In the morning Frank picked me up and we headed to retrieve blood tests from the doctor's office and then we were off to the courthouse to get that marriage license.

On Monday afternoon my bridesmaids and I attended a party at Judy and Ronald Jones' home. They lived about a block down the street from my folk's home, were fellow teachers, and wonderful friends to my family. At this party, we cut net into small squares then placed a teaspoonful of rice in the center of each square then brought the corners together, gave a small twist to the center then tied a small piece of ribbon around each one with a bow tied with the remaining ends of the ribbon.

My mom and my brother, Jimmy, went to Houston after school to get my wedding dress which had been left at a store in Houston to be altered.

My dad and my other three brothers were at my folks home hanging out. My brother, Grady, had a friend who had come over to visit and this friend had come for a visit riding a small motorcycle, probably the size of what we call a dirt bike today.

All was going smoothly according to plan. What could happen?

While my brother and his friend, who was visiting on Saturday, were in my folk's house, Frank and Jimmy had decided to hotwire my brother's friend's motorcycle and they rode it around the neighborhood. They were unaware that my brother, Mark, had been watching them and had learned from them how to hotwire the motorcycle.

So, Monday afternoon when, my brother's friend, Grady, had come back over to my folk's home again to visit, Mark decided to hotwire the motorcycle and take it for a ride. Since my mom and Jimmy had gone to Houston to pick up my wedding dress, Dad was home along with my three younger brothers. Frank had gone to his folk's house to help them while I was at the Jones' house making rice bags with my Bridesmaids.

My brother, Mark, who was thirteen-years-old at the time and a very quick learner and he was very successful at getting the motorcycle started. Mark then got on the motorcycle and took it for a ride but he lost control of it and ended up hitting a police car which was parked on the side of the road just a little way down the street from our house. When he hit the police car, the footrest of the motorcycle went through his leg causing a compound fracture in his calf the bone between his foot and knee.

My Dad and some other men quickly loaded Mark into a vehicle and rushed him to the hospital in Bay City which was about five miles away. My mom was with my oldest brother, Jimmy, in Houston picking up my wedding dress but could not be reached and would only find out when they returned home but Frank and I found out about what had happened when he picked me up from the Bridesmaids rice bag party shortly after the incident had happened.

Mark was supposed to be an usher in our wedding but that was not going to happen. Frank and I were just so glad that he was okay that we didn't even care.

My parents had some really good close friends that literally just took over and helped with the wedding while Mom and Dad were taking care of Mark at the hospital.

Sometimes we can't be prepared for events that happen in our lives but God always takes care of us in these times.

May 7, 1968, reality has set in and chaos was on its heels! The wedding rehearsal was planned for 5:00 p.m. All of the bridesmaids, groomsmen, ushers, the organist, and the preacher who could be in our wedding party were all at the church. The flower girl and ring-bearer were also there with their parents.

After a lively rehearsal with lots of laughter, everyone headed to the rehearsal dinner in Bay City.

Frank and I stopped by the hospital on our way to the rehearsal dinner to see Mark and give him our love and thank a friend of my parents who had volunteered to stay with Mark at the hospital so my folks could go to the rehearsal dinner. Mark was pretty sedated but he was glad we had come for a visit.

Frank and I gave gifts to the wedding party then we surprised each other with the secret gifts we had purchased for each other. Frank gave me a delicate pearl necklace with matching pearl earrings and I gave him a tie tack with a small diamond in it. Fifty years later, I still have these special gifts we gave each other that night. I never took the pearl necklace or the pearl earrings off until a few years ago when I noticed the pearls were getting worn down too much.

After the rehearsal dinner, Frank drove me home, held me in his arms, kissed me, and told me how much he loved me. I told him how much I loved him and to please not let them hurt him or drown him at the bachelor party which was to be held on the beach. Of course, knowing that the Three Muske-teers would be together again worried me! What could hap-pen? Absolutely anything! I would definitely not get much sleep that night.

Frank promised me he would not get hurt and would not let anything keep him from marrying me the next day.

17

going to the chapel

I tossed and turned all night trying to go to sleep but my restless mind would not stop thinking. The excitement and the anticipation that the next evening of becoming Frank's wife forever, just would not let my mind rest.

Of course, that was interlaced with worrisome thoughts about if Frank was okay. Knowing those guys all to well who had taken Frank to the beach for a bachelor party had me asking myself many questions. Did they let him drown? Was he tied up to a tree on the courthouse lawn in Bay City? Or worse yet, tied up to that tree in the nude? Had they used a chain and lost the padlock key?

Finally, I fell asleep but woke up in the middle of the night then set up quickly in the bed when I heard my brother Jimmy stumbling down the hall. I needed answers! Quickly, I got out of bed and ran into the hallway. Jimmy was startled but he laughed when he saw me. Questions and threats started flying out of my mouth as he looked at me in his hungover state.

"Is Frank okay? Did y'all tie or chain him to a tree somewhere? Where is the key? If, y'all hurt him, you're toast!"

Jimmy told me that Frank was alright, passed out but alright, and four of them had carried him by the arms and legs into his folk's house then put him in his bed. Jimmy said they had thought about tying him nude on top of his car then tell me he was sick so I would drive out there and find him but decided not to. Well now, that was just hunky-do kind of them! Why did his hungover words not make me feel better? As Jimmy walked away from me he also mumbled something about a case of vodka and gallons of orange juice. Good grief!

I went back to my room, got back in bed, tossed and turned for awhile praying then finally fell back to sleep but then got up later and went to the kitchen. While sitting at the kitchen bar, it seemed like forever, the phone rang.

When I answered it I heard, "Hey ,Nancy Lou, I love you! Get your bags packed, darling, because after lunch my brother is going to pick them up and bring them to my folk's house."

I asked him if he was alright and he assured me he was. I told him how much I loved him then he told me that he would be waiting at the altar for me.

Worry had been replaced by total excitement and I danced around the room singing "Going to the Chapel and we're going to get married!"

There was much to do but total excitement surrounded me. I packed my suitcase then took it to the front hall to wait for Frank's brother to pick it up then I headed to the shower to start the process of getting ready. It was already after lunch and the time was flying by. When I came out of the bathroom from my shower, my suitcase had been picked up which somehow made the reality of the day even more real.

The wedding party was to be at the church at before 5:00 p.m. to get dressed and take pictures. Since I was doing my own hair and makeup, I had to get busy and I did. Time flew by then I was driven to the church with my wedding dress, veil, and shoes with me.

Arriving at the church, I was led to a large room where my bridesmaids and I would get dressed for the wedding. They were all there dressed and waiting for me. The excitement in the room was surreal with lots of laughter as they helped me especially as we tried to get the hoop pulled up that would hold out the skirt of my wedding dress. That "thang" was unbelievable!

The photographer took pre-wedding pictures of me and the bridesmaids, my dad and I, and my mom and I. Frank and the groomsmen also took pictures in a separate room, so we would not see each other before the wedding.

After the pictures were taken, the bridesmaids and I returned to our dressing room and waited. Many people came to give hugs and their love. My grandmother, Ninnie, loaned me her pearl necklace to wear as something old and borrowed which I wore with my single pearl necklace Frank had given me the night before as something new, my garter had blue on it for something blue, and my Dad made sure I had a sixpence in my shoe.

Slowly the bridesmaids left the room one at a time to proceed down the aisle with a groomsman to the front of the church. When the last of them left, my dad sweetly kissed me on the cheek telling he loved me, I was beautiful, then he gently covered my face with the shorter veil. The wedding march music, "Here Comes the Bride," began then Dad took my arm in his, told me he loved me again, and we walked slowly down the aisle to the front of the church.

The church was totally packed with friends and family who all rose to there feet when the music began.

When dad and I got to the end of the aisle, the preacher asked who gave this woman in marriage to this man and dad said, "Her mother and I," then he gently took the short veil covering my face and lifted it over my head placing it on top of and with the longer veil behind my pearl tiara. Dad had tears in his eyes as he gently kissed my cheek again and slightly stumbled as he took his place in the front pew with my mom.

My dad and I were very close. Out of five children, I was the only girl and daddy always called me "his sweetheart." My dad was the first man I ever loved with all of my heart and on this day he had just given me with his blessings to be married to the man I would love for eternity with all of my heart. This is not an easy task for a dad and the emotion overwhelmed my daddy.

My maid of honor, Gwen Gelber, helped me up the two steps to place where Frank was standing, smiling with those big ol' dimples, then she took my bouquet from me. I turned to face Frank and I could not stop smiling.

Frank and I exchanged vows, rings, and a beautiful sweet kiss, then he took my hand and we walked hand in hand back down that aisle as Mr. and Mrs. Loren Frank Henderson, Jr.

We took more pictures immediately following the wedding with the entire wedding party and our parents at the church while our guest left to go to the reception at the Oasis Motel in Bay City, Texas which was ready for their arrival. When the photographer was finished with the pictures we headed to the reception but took a few minutes for the groomsmen to load me in the car because of that ridiculous hoop under the skirt of my wedding dress. I thought for sure that they would totally expose me to themselves and the whole world but thank God that did not happen!

18

wedding reception

As Jimmy, our chauffeur and best man, drove Frank and I up to the wedding reception at the Oasis Hotel, we noticed that they had put our names on their lighted marque in front of the hotel saying, "Frank and Nancy Wedding Reception." It was so special! It would be the first and last time we ever had our names in lights but that made it even more special.

Jimmy pulled the car up to the front door entrance then Frank and Jimmy helped me to get out of the car without the "hoop thangy" exposing me to all of the guests who were waiting for our arrival. The lobby was full of people as we made our way through it saying hello then going to the winding metal staircase that led upstairs to the large wedding reception room.

The photographer was there and ushered us to the table that held the wedding cake and punch. It was so beautiful with the cake sat on one end of a long table which was covered with a linen tablecloth and the crystal punch bowl full of punch sat on the opposite end. In the center of the table sat a sterling silver candelabra holding five tall white candles that had already been lit.

The photographer took pictures of Frank and I cutting the wedding cake, feeding it to each other, and drinking punch from our two stemmed glasses with intertwined arms which actually was the only cake and punch we had. My little brother Mark, who was in a wheelchair from the motorcycle injury, was already in the room along with the hostesses and our parents.

Being the big sister, I served Mark a piece of the wedding cake and a glass of punch before Frank and I went to the door where the guests would enter the room. We stood there with our grandmothers standing on either side of us shaking hands, hugging and greeting the guests as they went to be served cake and punch. Soon the room was full of people and laughter.

The strangest thing though, I do not remember seeing the two of the Three Musketeers or Frank's other buddies from the bachelor party. Maybe I just missed them as they went through the greeting line?

Soon all of the guests had been greeted then served punch and cake.

My best friend and maid of honor, Gwen Gelber, came and told me it was time to go to a small room which had been designated as a place for me to change out of my wedding dress into a going away suit that my parents had bought for me to leave for the honeymoon.

Frank and I had decided to forgo the removing of my garter in front our guest because of that hoop thangy that would have definitely sprung up over my head if I had even wanted to sit down. Frank would just have to throw it only after I took it off in the small changing room. Never ever wear one of those hoop thangies, just trust me on that!

After changing clothes with Gwen's help, we went back into the reception room and the corsage from the center of my bouquet was taken out then pinned on my suit by Gwen. When Frank came to my side, I handed him the garter as Gwen handed me my bouquet then she ran down the stairs to the lobby to get ready for me to toss the bouquet.

Frank and I left the reception room through the door which we had entered it then walked to the landing at the top of the stairs. I threw my bouquet down into the lobby of guests and Gwen caught it. Frank threw the garter into the crowd below then grabbed my hand and said, "Let's go, Nancy Lou!"

We ran down the steps as fast as we could then out of the back door of the lobby followed by everyone. When we got outside we were pelted with rice as we dodged and ducked through the crowd. I was laughing, Frank was laughing, and we held each other's hand tightly as we ran but then out of nowhere we heard loud footsteps running behind us!

Suddenly, one of Frank's bachelor party buddies ran past us to Frank's car, opened the hood of the car, and began to pull all of the spark plug wires off of the engine! At the nearly the same time, Frank was pulled from my hand and hoisted up into the air then carried away quickly by five more of his buddies as they ran carrying him to the back of the hotel. They were followed, of course, by all of our running and laughing guests!

I stood there a minute in shock then I ran quickly in the direction they had carried Frank. As I got to the back of the hotel, I saw them throw Frank in his Army dress uniform into the swimming pool. A loud roar of laughter came out of the crowd, then I laughed too.

I ran to the edge of the pool laughing as Frank climbed out on to the edge then stood next to me. Frank picked me up into his arms and with a big ol' dimpled smile on his face held me over the water as if threatening to drop me into the swimming pool.

Everyone had gathered around us and were encouraging Frank but before he could put me back on the ground, my brother, Jimmy pushed us both into the swimming pool! My mom who was just a tad upset then walked over and pushed Jimmy into the swimming pool too. Of course, laughter rang out all around us.

Standing there in the swimming pool, looking like a soaking wet bride in my "going away suit", and wearing my new kid leather shoes under the water, I watched as Jimmy and Frank took turns going up the ladder of the high diving board and jumping off doing cannonballs trying to spray our guests with water.

My daddy was laughing really hard, that is until my mom told him how much she had spent on my shoes. Those shoes were never the same after that! Soft leather should never become crunchy.

Finally, Jimmy exited the pool then Frank swam to me and helped me out of the pool. We dried off as much as possible then headed to Frank's car but as we approached the car, suddenly Frank grabbed my hand told me to run, then we ran as fast as we could to his parent's car, jumped in, and since the keys were in the ignition, Frank started the car then off we drove quickly.

Frank was driving very fast and taking every back road he knew to shake anyone who might be following us! We were both laughing when Frank told me we needed to get out of the wet clothes we were wearing. We decided the best place to go was his folks' house which was out in the country about nine miles from Bay City and we were already on Old Van Vleck Road that led to his folk's house.

After arriving at the driveway of Frank's folk's home. Frank quickly got out of the car opened the garage door then ran back got into the car, pulled the car into the open garage, got out quickly, and pulled the garage door down behind the car.

Frank had a key to the house, so he unlocked the door told me to go inside but to leave the lights off. Frank went back to the car and came into the house carrying our suitcases which shocked me to see that our suitcases were in his hands. Frank told me that the plan was to use his folk's car for our Honeymoon the whole time because he and his dad were sure that Frank's car would get really messed up at the wedding reception.

I stared at Frank as he looked at me with our suitcases in his hands then as if he could read my mind and heart he said, "Nancy, I am going to take your suitcase to my old room so you can change your clothes there and I am going to change clothes in my folk's room."

Even though we were married, at least for a few hours, we would wait for that special moment, in a special place which would be memorable to our hearts.

Just as we came out of our separate dressing rooms, we heard a car coming down the driveway. Frank grabbed our suitcases and we both ran to the door we had entered from the garage. Frank put the suitcases back in the trunk of the car but just as I was getting ready to get in the car while Frank opened the garage door, we heard familiar voices which were those of his parents. They had just returned from the wedding reception, so we chatted with them for a while.

Frank's dad told us that they had left Lloyd, Frank's brother, and his steady girlfriend, Theresa, in the parking lot at the Oasis Hotel to get the ice out of the front seat which had been piled high up above the windows by the "Bachelor Party Crew" and Lloyd was going to try to get the spark plugs back on the engine in the right order. Frank, Lloyd and their Dad had always worked on cars together and each of their cars had been fixed by them at some point, so Lloyd knew what he was doing all too well. Frank and I still owe them for that favor.

Frank's dad's words were, "Son, your car is a mess! Thank goodness we made other plans for your honeymoon vehicle!" Probably not his exact words but the gist of what he said.

It was already getting to be very late when Frank and I left his folk's home, so we drove to Alvin which was only about fifty miles from their home then stopped at the Holiday Inn. Frank went in and got us a room while I waited in the car. When he returned we drove to the side of the Inn that our room was located on, parked the car then went up the stairs to the landing on the second floor where our room was. Frank unlocked the door then picked me up into his arms and carried me across the threshold before he went back to the car to get our suitcases. I watched him from the doorway until he returned, and then when he entered the room again we shut the door.

Just like in the beautiful song that was sung at our wedding, "Whither Thou Goest," I knew that I would always go with Frank where ever he went. We were one heart and soul married to each other in the laws of man and in the eyes of God with His love and blessings for eternity.

19

honeymoon

Waking up that first morning as Frank's wife was surreal. Wondering was it all a dream or reality, then I heard Frank say, "Good morning, Mrs. L. F. Henderson, Jr." and I knew it was real.

Frank and I did what we needed to do to get dressed then repacked our suitcases so we could get a start on our first day as husband and wife.

I should stop right here and say thank you with very deep appreciation to my mom and her good friend, Peggy Goodloe Fisher. Evidently, they were feeling very mischievous while I was in the shower the day of my wedding, so they sprinkled a huge bag of rice into my suitcase which I thought I could entrust them with while it was sitting safely and securely in the front hallway of my parent's home. As they planned and anticipated, the rice did get into every crease and cranny of every piece of clothing in my suitcase! May 9, 1968, would be the beginning of a rice trail my suitcase would leave across Texas.

Frank and I did not have a planned out honeymoon. This was totally a part of Frank's beautiful personality: he loved to just get in a car then head out without a plan then stop and explore along the way. So when we left the Holiday Inn, we headed North on Highway 35 towards Houston, Texas then kept on going.

As we drove, Frank and I were talking about our wedding and discussing who was there when Frank remembered that his uncle from DeSoto, Texas had not been able to come to the wedding. Since we were only a few miles from DeSoto during that part of our conversation, Frank and I decided to pay him a visit.

Frank's Uncle was very surprised when we walked into the bank where he was working. Frank introduced me to his uncle and he told us that he would like to take us out for supper. When Frank's uncle closed the bank, we all headed to his home. He was really excited to see us and told us that he wanted us to stay the night at his home so we could all go out to eat, visit, and not feel rushed.

Frank's uncle took us to a steakhouse in Dallas to eat supper which was absolutely an amazing place. He ordered filet mignon steak for me. I had never eaten filet mignon but it has been forever ingrained in my mind now and just how awesome it was but it still took second place to meeting and visiting with my new uncle which was just wonderful.

The next morning early, we all had breakfast together then Frank and I got back on the road again. This time we headed towards Dallas, Texas. Frank was a big history fan and wanted to see the book depository in Dealey Plaza where supposedly a single gunman had shot and killed President John F. Kennedy from a window. We parked and walked in front of that building, talking about what had happened there, and coming to our own conclusions then we left and headed towards Arlington, Texas where we spent our third night at a Caravan Motel.

The next morning we headed towards San Antonio, Texas stopping along the way looking in shops. We stopped in Waco, Texas to eat lunch at a place called The Chicken Shack then we continued our drive towards San Antonio but stopped just north of there at a Rodeway Inn because it had gotten late in the evening.

By now you are probably thinking I have a really great memory. Absolutely not, I just have memorabilia that Frank had saved and put into that "Magical Cedar Chest" for me to be led to find forty-seven years later.

The next morning we got up early and drove into San Antonio. While on our drive Frank told me that we were going to the HemisFair which was the Official 1968 World's

Fair. I was totally surprised and really excited as he was telling me about it. Our first priority was to find a place to stay. We looked for the famous Tower of the Americas which we did finally see rising high in the skyline above the city of San Antonio then headed in its direction.

Of course, we got lost. San Antonio is a city where the roads seem to go in circles. We were without a map so we stopped and bought one at a filling station. After traveling in circles and ending up at dead ends, we decided that we were close enough to the HemisFair to arrive there early the next morning. We rented a room at a Travelodge where we would stay for the duration of our Honeymoon.

We spent the rest of the day just hanging out at the swimming, eating Oreo cookies which we had bought at a little store close by, making plans for the next day, and watching TV in our room but for the life of me, I can not remember what we watched on TV.

The next day we got up early and headed for the Hemis-Fair which we finally made it to after driving in several circles following the roads listed on the map. We spent the whole day there. We rode the elevator to the top of the Tower of the Americas where we ate lunch at the restaurant while we took in the view as the restaurant revolved letting us see a panoramic sweep of the Texas countryside then we rode the elevator back down and walked through the fair.

Frank won for me a blue teddy bear at one of the game places along the pathway through the booths then he bought me a small winding grandfather's clock with a key which is only eight inches tall and was made in Germany. It still works and I still have it fifty years later.

After a full day of walking around the HemisFair and enjoying everything there, we went back to the Travelodge. The next morning was Mother's Day so after breakfast, we called our moms and wished them a happy Mother's Day then we decided it would be fun to visit the Alamo.

After we visited the Alamo we went out to eat at a nice restaurant then headed back to the Travelodge to eat Oreo cookies and watch TV. Sorry, I just don't remember what we watched on TV.

The next morning Frank and I loaded up our luggage, mine, of course, nearly empty of rice, and headed back to Van Vleck, Texas where we would have less than six days together before Frank would leave for his new Army training in at Fort Devens in Ayer, Massachusetts

Frank and I had made a decision that would not be very popular with others but we decided that I would start attending school again after he left for Ayer, Mass., knowing that I could make up the work I would miss at school but not wanting to spend one minute away from Frank until I had to.

20

separation hurts deeply

F rank and I arrived back to Van Vleck from our honeymoon on May 13, 1968, which meant we needed to decide where we were going to stay. We decided to split the time he had left of his leave staying together at our folk's homes. Frank would fly out for Fort Devens in Ayer, Massachusetts on May 18, 1968, but I would not be able to follow him there until June 1, 1968, the day after I graduated from High School.

We spent every minute of those few days together but it seemed like the minutes flew by too quickly then suddenly it was time to take Frank to the airport for him to fly away by himself leaving me watching as his plane took flight

This would be our first separation as a married couple. The daytimes were not as bad but my hand felt empty without him holding it with his but both of our days were filled with being around other people, The nights held many tears from my eyes as I cried into my pillow missing him lying next to me where God had meant him to be.

Frank was struggling with the same feelings that I was having and in this next letter and he will share them with you himself.

> *May 19, 1968*
> *Dear Wife,*
> *I hate to say this but big brave soldier me almost broke down and shed a few tears yesterday. I have never felt so lonely and bad before. When I left this time I didn't leave my girl, I left someone who is a part of me, my darling wife.*
> *Nancy those last two weeks we have spent together were the most beautiful two weeks in my life. Last night I couldn't sleep because there was no one's head on my shoulder and when I woke up this morning you weren't*

there and it felt so strange. I can't wait until you get up here and we can set up our own house together and start a family if you want to.

Darling, I want you to go out to my folk's house Friday night and I'll call you there. It will be between 7:00 and 10:00 p.m. If I don't call don't worry because I might have detail or KP. If I don't call Friday, I'll call Sunday about 2:00 p.m. Okay?

You should start packing your things and mine too. Get Mom to help you with mine because she knows what all fits and all. Is your Dad going to bring you up or what? I'm am going to look for a place next weekend and it'll be waiting for you. Please hurry.

Did you get your lessons caught up? You better have. Are you getting excited about graduation? I don't have an address yet but I should have on by the time I call so you can send up the Marriage License. Do you still want to be my wife? You realize, of course, that it's going to be tuff for a long time and we may not have much or be able to do much? Well take care and Hurry! I LOVE MY WIFE!

All My Love,
Frank
P.S. Wife, I love you and miss you terribly!

Frank mailed the above letter written on May 19, 1968, along with another letter written to me on May 21, 1968, both were postmarked May 21, 1968. They would arrive the same day but had actually been written two days apart. I think he missed me. I know I was missing him.

Dear Wife,
Well, what's the hold-up? Get your butt up here! This weekend I'm going with my buddy to try and find a

THE LOVE STORY OF NANCY & FRANK

place to live for us. There aren't many so don't be disappointed if we have a hole. Okay?

Get my Dad to draw all the money I have out of the Credit Union and all the money I have in the bank out and bring it with you, we'll need every cent. I have an address you can send the license to and I need it now badly, make sure it has a raised seal and if it doesn't take it to a notary republic. This is my buddy's address and keep writing me there (if you so desire) until I get a permanent address because he will bring the mail to me from their apartment. Have your things ready to go and if you can come on up Saturday.

Do you know yet how you are coming? If you're flying, find out how much it will cost to ship everything up and how long it will take to get here. Darling, I miss you so much already. Friday, we are supposed to ship our permanent barracks and start school Monday. But by the next weekend, I should be living with my wife and I'll be so happy!

Get Mom and Dad to help you with my things and financial standings. Tell my folks I'll be writing soon and I'll be calling Sunday night to talk to you and them. So, I am going to close for now and get some rest because tomorrow night we have a GI party. So, take care and remember I love you and need you up here as soon as possible.

All My Love,
Frank
P.S. Tell everyone hi.
P.S. I Love My Wife.

Frank included his friend's address in this letter but I chose not to include the address or his buddy's name.

Frank needed our marriage license to give to the Army so we could apply for our allotment which would be for our off-base housing and food. As with all things, it would take time for the Army to process the paperwork for the allotment which you will read about in a future chapter of this book.

The next letter is the one that I wrote back to Frank answering some of his questions and telling him my plans.

May 23, 1968

Dearest Husband,

Hi Sweetheart! First of all, I want to say I miss you, and I'm going out of my mind because I Love You so much and I can't see you until Saturday, June 1, 1968, in exactly eight days but probably four or five days from when you get this letter. Honey, I'm sending you the Marriage License right away with this letter. I will send it Airmail so maybe you'll get it sooner.

Honey, I don't care what the place looks like that we live in as long as it's a place to live and ESPECIALLY be with you. Frank every night I cry, I just miss you being by my side so much. You belong next to me and for you to be gone is terrible. I Love You, Frank. Mrs. L. F. Henderson, Jr. says I Love You to Mr. L. F. Henderson, Jr. I miss you so much.

I'm coming up there on a plane and I'm leaving June 1st probably about the same time you left. Are you going to meet me, I hope so because I'll be lost if you don't. I'm freighting our things and probably some of our clothes because I can't carry too much on the plane. I'm coming by student fare which is 1/3 off. It will cost me about $70. I think Mom and Dad will probably buy my ticket. Grandma gave me $25 more dollars today. I'll draw *out all of your money and put it in Travelers Checks so I won't lose it.*

Guess what is on the radio? "Yummy, Yummy, Yummy, I've got love in my Tummy", and I do! Love just for you! Honey, I'll be at you folks house Friday night and I'll be so happy to hear your voice that I'll probably cry. Our little clock is still just a ticking! I wind it every day and it hasn't ever messed up.

I've caught up on most of my homework except for Physics, but maybe that hard ole Dad, Mr. Blakley will give me a break. Honey, I'll have to close for now it's getting late and I'm still doing makeup work. Honey, I Love You and I'll always want to be your Wife, no matter what!

All My Love,

Nancy

Mrs. L. F. Henderson, Jr.

Your Wife!

P.S. XXXXXXXXXXXXXXXXX Kisses! Just a fraction of what you'll get when I get there! Love Nancy

Frank would call collect to his folk's house on Sunday, May 26, 1968, and we got to talk to each other on the phone long distance. Six days later on the morning of June 1, 1968, after I graduated from high school the night before, I would fly out on an airplane by myself to go live with Frank in Ayer, Massachusetts. It would be the first time I had ever flown on an airplane and, of course, there would be some glitches along the way.

21

first home

Getting on an airplane in Houston at Hobby Airport then being nervous because of never having flown before, I so was excited to finally be on my way to be with Frank again.

Of course, flying student stand-by meant that I could be held up at any point of my trip if the plane I was scheduled to fly on was full with others who had paid the full amount for a ticket. My flight would take me from Houston to Chicago then after changing planes in Chicago, I would fly on to Boston where Frank would be waiting at the airport for me.

After arriving at the airport in Chicago and finally finding the gate for my connecting flight to Boston, an announcement was made at the gate that the plane was full and all those with student stand-by tickets would have to wait for the next plane. Needless to say, I was in panic mode. What should I do? How would I let Frank know? Would Frank be going nuts waiting in Boston?

Frank had asked me to bring all of the money he had saved before we married along with me. I had put this money in travelers checks, so I went to the desk then asked the woman there how much it would cost for me to upgrade to the full ticket price. After finding out the cost, I paid her to upgrade my ticket so as to be able to get on the next plane.

When the plane that I was supposed to be on landed in Boston without me on it, Frank called my folk's house collect to find out where I was. When my dad finished talking with Frank, in a panic he called the Chicago airport and had them page me to call home. That was all good, except dad had them page me as "Nancy Blakley" instead of "Nancy Henderson" which was funny later but did not matter at the time because I had already loaded on to the next plane to Boston.

To make this all even more surreal, the plane I loaded on to had been brought specially to the gate because of the number of people with student stand-by tickets that could not load on the previous plane. So, I totally wasted some of our money.

When I arrived at the Boston Airport, Frank was there waiting for me. A buddy, who had been in basic training with Frank, and his wife had driven Frank to the airport from Ayer, Massachusetts which was thirty miles from Boston. We got my bags then loaded up in their car for the ride to our new home.

On the way, we stopped at the commissary on Fort Devens base to pick up some groceries. I could not go in because of not having an ID yet to get in the door. So while Frank and his buddy went inside, his buddy's wife and I stayed in the car. I forgot to tell Frank to get some foil, but when telling his buddy's wife, she looked confused then asked me if Frank would know what I needed if she told him what I had just said. I told her of course, then she asked me to spell "foil" and she immediately started laughing. Seems my spoken foil word sounded like "fall"! This couple was from Iowa and said foil with two syllables which sounded to me like "fall-ill." We all got a big laugh out of the way I talk. Until that conversation, I had no idea that I even had an accent.

Frank had rented us an apartment about two miles outside of Ayer, Massachusetts on Sandy Pond Road, which was the only apartment that was available at the time. The rent was $100.^{00} a month but did not include electricity. This was pretty expensive since Frank's pay was only $60.^{00} a month but he had just applied for my allotment which would be an extra $100.^{00} a month. I had brought traveler's checks with me in the amount of $150.^{00} which was all of Frank's savings but had spent $25.^{00} of that money upgrading my flight. We also figured the allotment money would start soon.

The apartment building looked a lot like an army barracks that had been moved there and made into apartments. Our apartment was on the left end of the building and upstairs. We had a bedroom, living room, kitchen, and bathroom. At the bottom of the building, there was a screen door which opened to a small foyer which had a staircase going up leading to another small landing with the front door of our apartment.

After passing through the front door you entered a long hallway which had a sloping ceiling with a cubby hole on the left side of the hall with a window which when opened then laid back up on to the roof on the right side of the hall where there were two doors. The first door went into our bedroom and the next door went into the living room. Once in the living room if you turned left another door led to our kitchen.

The bathroom door was to the left as you entered the kitchen and had a ceiling that gradually sloped down from the bathroom door to the bathtub. This sloping ceiling held a window that opened up and laid back up on to the roof. Only one side of the roof of the building had been extended out from the roof to make more ceiling height space for the kitchen, living room, and bedroom.

Our apartment did not have air conditioning or heating and we didn't have any ceiling fans or as a matter of fact any type of a fan. Also, it didn't come with a washer, dryer, or dishwasher.

We did not have a telephone, TV, or a car. What we did have, was each other which was the only thing we really needed and the most important thing to us.

The apartment building was within walking distance of Sandy Pond which looked like a small lake and in its center there was a floating wooden platform that you could swim out to, sit on it, or dive off.

There was also a small convenience store about three blocks from our apartment house. Since we could only go to the commissary once a month because of the expense of a cab or by bumming a ride with a friend with a car, we would pick up small things at that little store.

At the commissary, we bought a lot of powdered things such as instant milk and potatoes. Also canned items such as ham, potted meat, tuna, canned milk, and vegetables of all kinds. Our refrigerator had only a ten-inch by ten-inch cube that hung from the inside top that was considered the freezer it would only hold two small metal ice trays and maybe four one-pound packages of hamburger which limited the number of fresh meats we could buy and freeze.

When beginning to write this book of love and memories of Frank and I, these memories came to my mind in beautiful fun stories of the things that we had done together. I chose to give these stories special titles. Since this experience was such a fun way for me to reminisce about these memories, I have decided to share our love story through these fun and beautiful memory stories.

"Sail away with us to another world as we rely on each other as we ride it together."

22

dive bombers

A fter arriving at our apartment house, I was not really sure who was most excited, Frank or me. After opening the screen door, we ran up the stairs to a front door to enter into our new home. We had arms full of bags of groceries and were followed closely behind by our friends who had their arms full of groceries, too.

As Frank opened our door, he looked at me smiling saying, "Welcome home, Nancy Lou."

I went past Frank smiling, laughing, then looking into the first open doorway to our right as we all walked down a long hallway to another door which we entered then I saw a kitchen through the next doorway. After running to put bags of groceries down on the kitchen table, I just stood there taking it all in. It was my very first kitchen as Frank's wife. I loved it and I loved him.

Our friends helped us put the groceries away, we thanked them for everything, then they left us to get settled in. Frank showed me everything he had already done to the apartment. Our things that I had shipped had not arrived yet but Frank had bought some things to get us through until they arrived.

Frank and I had such a magical and memorable first night in our new home as every day and night would be for us as we grew to be one heart and soul for eternity. God had truly blessed us with an unbridled love for each other as we went on our journey together.

Since it was summertime in Massachusetts it was really hot and humid. Frank and I did not have any sort of fan, so we moved our head-board-less bed under the only window in our bedroom. Our pillows were lined up under the window so that when we laid down on the bed our heads would be the closest thing to the open window hoping to get as much of a breeze as possible.

One night as we laid in bed sweating and praying for a breeze, mosquitoes seemed to be not only buzzing outside the window but they were coming through the screen into the bedroom. They did not just come in as a few but it seemed like by the hundreds. I don't know what those screens on the windows were made out of but it seemed to me that it had to be chicken wire because they were not stopping one mosquito!

Now, I know that you all know that sound a mosquito makes when it is "dive bombing" at your head and believe me these dudes were in full dive bombing mode. We tried to put the sheet over our heads but the sound was unreal.

All of a sudden, Frank jumped out of the bed, flipped on the light, then grabbed his pillow, and pulled the pillowcase off. He smiled showing those awesome dimples of his then started swatting mosquitoes with his pillowcase. Well now, since I was his forever "shotgun wife," I grabbed my pillow, pulled the pillowcase off, stood on the bed, started swatting mosquitoes on the ceiling, laughed, and jumped up and down on the bed.

Frank evidently thought that looked like fun, so he joined me on the bed and we both swatted mosquitoes while we jumped up and down on the bed. We were swatting blood sucking, dive bombing mosquitoes and laughing really loudly when we realized that it was in the middle of the night. Also, we remembered that we lived upstairs and that there was an apartment below us.

Oops! Everyone in the apartment house knew that we were newlyweds and they surely had figured out that we were very, very young and energetic. Of course, that just made Frank and I laugh harder because we knew the neighbors had no idea that we were just swatting mosquitoes.

Finally, we decided that we had enough of the swatting and we put new pillowcases on the pillows, laid back down and we're just fixing to drift off to sleep when a strong breeze started coming through the window. God had decided to give us a nice breeze as a reward for our efforts.

We had solved the mosquito problem together for at least one night.

Although the mosquitoes would never really go away, the biggest problem was getting a breeze to help us sleep and keep us from sweating to death at night. It was not so bad in the apartment during the day because I could open the windows that flipped back up on to the roof which helped draw the air through the apartment.

We could not open those windows at night because they did not have screens. The mosquitoes seemed to come out after dark so the screen-less windows had to be closed.

Frank always left early to go to Fort Devens for school since we did not have a car. He walked the three miles to the base then after he got out of his Morse Code Interceptor classes he would walk the three miles home.

It was a Friday morning and I had told Frank before he left for school that there would be cookies waiting for him when he got home that evening. Knowing that the cookies would need to be made in the morning because of the temperature rising outside and inside our apartment during the afternoon, I decided to get busy making them. It is said that heat rises and since we lived in an upstairs apartment, I really believe that was true.

While thinking about the temperature rising in our apartment during the day, I got out my trusty hand-held electric mixer then put one of the beaters into its slot. Suddenly, I did not see it as a mixer anymore but a gonna be fan! I was in invention mode but now I needed something to make some fan blades out of.

Looking around the room, I spotted the Corn Flakes cereal box. Perfect! I got a large bowl out of the cabinet, emptied the cereal into the bowl, got out my scissors, and cut four beautifully shaped blades out of the cardboard cereal box then attached the blades to the single beater's four rung thangys with masking tape. Of course, being excited Nancy Lou did a happy dance but I was not done yet.

Foil, the foil would make the blades of my "beater-fan" look awesome, so I covered each blade with foil, plugged in the mixer turned fan then turned the mixer on, and that dude worked! Now all I had to do was wait for Frank to come home to show him my new invention.

Frank was whistling as he came up the drive to our apartment house and I ran out to meet him. Excitedly I told him about making the beater-fan, as we walked up the stairs to our apartment. Of course, Frank loved it when I showed it to him.

That night we placed the beater-fan on the window sill above our heads then turned it on. It really worked well and before long we both fell asleep under the cool breeze from the fan.

Suddenly, in the middle of the night, the beater-fan attacked us! The fan had vibrated off of the window sill then landed between our heads, slapping us with its blades, grabbing at the pillowcases, bouncing around, and making an awful noise.

Frank jumped out of the bed and pulled the plug on that fan. Frank smiled at me as he laughed saying, "Nancy Lou, I think we are gonna have to tape that dude down!"

So, of course, we got the masking tape then after a few repairs to the gone wild beater-fan, Frank taped it down to the window sill.

Of course, this was just the beginning of the Frank and Nancy Henderson duo escapades.

23

clothes, oreos, candy lipsticks

F rank and I solved our fan problem with our beater fan, or at least for awhile. Now we began to settle into a daily routine.

On the weekdays we got up before dawn because Frank needed to be at Fort Devens early in the morning for his classes. Since we did not have a car and it was a three-mile walk to the base for him, he started out early on his walk to the base.

After Frank left for school, I had things to do which kept me busy and fueled my special inventiveness. I loved figuring out a better way of doing things while making do with what we had.

Dishes had been washed and it was time for me to start the process of washing our clothes. While listening to music on the radio, I sang and danced around the kitchen. We had a little transistor radio that I had brought with me from Texas when I had flown to Ayer, Massachusetts. Music and dancing had always been part of the spiritual soul in me and, of course, Frank love his dancing Nancy Lou.

After separating our clothes by light, dark, and white colors, I filled the kitchen sink with hot water then added the powdered clothes soap, while swishing it around in the hot water so it would dissolve. The kitchen sink was a big rectangle and shallow so it could not hold very many clothes at one time. I put some of the smaller items into the sink, scrubbed them between my fisted hands then wrung them out twisting them with hands then placed them on the counter while emptying the sink of the soapy water.

When the sink was empty, I placed the wet clothes back in the sink and rinsed them with water one at a time. After wringing each item out they were put in the clothes basket then I picked up the basket, walked through the kitchen door into the living room, through the living room into the hall, walked down the hall to the front door which was open to the landing, ran down the stairs to the screen door, opened it, and headed to the clothesline. Once the clothes were all hung on the clothesline, I returned to the kitchen to begin again.

While refilling the kitchen sink, thoughts came to me that this was going to take lots of filling, emptying, wringing, rinsing, and trips up and down that "dag-nabbit" staircase. Suddenly a light bulb came on in my head! Bathtub! The bathtub was huge and it would hold a lot of clothes at one time!

So, to the bathroom, I went with all of the clothes, detergent, bleach, radio, and the clothes basket. After filling the bathtub with hot water then swished detergent and clothes then I got down on my knees, leaned over the side of the tub, and started scrubbing the clothes. A great song came on the radio and dancing came to my mind when another light bulb came on in my head, I could just get into the tub then boogie dance those clothes clean. Of course, that is exactly what I did and when they seemed boogie-danced enough, the tube was emptied, clothes rinsed, wrung out, and then put in the clothes basket.

The only problem that came up after that, was the basket was too heavy to carry. I pushed/pulled the basket through the house until getting to the staircase then stopped. There was absolutely no way of carrying that basket full of wet clothes down the stairs because it was too heavy. I sat down on the platform at the top of the stairs when I saw the solution!

The staircase had a concave thangy going on in the center of it all the way to its bottom, most likely from people going up and down it for years. Laughing, I ran down the stairs, latched the screen door, ran back up the stairs, sat down on the top platform, drug the clothes basket until it was in front of me, straddled it, lined it up with the middle of the stairs and with a push sailed that dude down the staircase.

The basket sailed down the stairs like a sailboat and stopped when it ran into the screen door. Happy dance! I ran down the stairs, went around the basket, unlatched the screen door, drug that basket full of boogie clothes to the clothesline and hung the clothes out to dry.

After repeating this whole process one more time the clothes were all on the clothesline to dry. Of course, I would have to go down then wring the water out of the bottom of the clothes a few times. Evidently, I wasn't a very good wringer but I was one fantastic boogie dancing sailor!

The weeks would pass as Frank and I shared our love with each other but as with all things, we would come against a very unexpected difficult time. The allotment we had applied for with the Army got delayed and we found ourselves short of money for food after we had paid the rent and utilities.

We had been in Ayer, Massachusetts for two months but for some reason, our allotment from the Army had not started coming in Frank's pay. We had been fine until the third-month rent came due because I had brought of $150 with me but now that was all gone. Frank only got $60 a month from the Army and our rent was $100 which we paid plus utilities.

We paid the rent and utilities but were left with very little money left for food. Frank and I made it scraping along for about two weeks but then the reality of running out of food hit. We were down to a can of peas, flour, yeast, mustard, sugar, crackers, and a can of spam. The cupboard and refrigerator were empty except for those things.

Since Frank was on the base during the weekdays, he could eat breakfast and lunch there which was good because he was walking the three miles to the base those days. He was trying to bring anything nonperishable that he could acquire at the mess hall home, to help out with us having food to eat at supper time. During the day unknown to Frank, I was just drinking enormous amounts of water with a few crackers to save food for supper. When Frank figured out on the weekend what I was doing during the weekdays, of course, he was not very happy with me but I explained to him that I was not walking six miles a day and it was more important for him to have food.

Our evening meal consisted of a pizza-like crust made from flour, yeast, and water then after kneading and rolling out, I spread on mustard, added some mashed peas, then some cubed spam. These pizzas were absolutely awful but they were food and filling. Frank was a smoker, so in the evenings we walked along the roadside picking up cigarette butts, stripping them down, taking the tobacco out, and then he would roll the tobacco in a piece of paper from envelopes then smoke those cigarettes. I know that sounds awful but it is true. Desperate times are not good times to stop smoking.

Our special friends who took us to buy groceries once a month on the base and who had driven Frank to the airport to pick me up when I arrived in Massachusetts, invited Frank and me to there house for supper the night before payday. They were older than us and had taken us under their wings to help. We had grilled cheese sandwiches and I do believe those were the best grilled sandwiches I have ever eaten.

Finally, payday arrived! From our kitchen window, I heard Frank walking up the driveway whistling and singing. I ran to meet him when he picked me up swinging me around saying, "Nancy Lou, we have money and our allotment has been added to my pay including the previous two months. We are rich!" I couldn't quit smiling as we ran up the stairs together.

Frank changed into civilian clothes then said, "Let's go to the little store down the road and buy some food."

We ran down those stairs then we ran to that little store and we bought Oreo cookies and candy lipsticks. What can I say? We were both eighteen and full of fun! The next day we would buy real food but that night we would be young and foolish.

24

big fins

A fter having survived the two weeks of not enough food, Frank and I realized that we would have to manage our money very carefully. Frank was in constant search for another apartment for us because of the high rent we were paying. Also, he wanted to get closer to town and Fort Devens but for now we were enjoying our apartment in the country.

We were only blocks away from a small lake which was called Sandy Pond which was beautiful with a beach and a floating platform that we could swim to. Swimming in the pond was free, so Frank and I went there on the weekends sometimes to enjoy the beauty of it and swim.

Since Frank was in Morse code school, he would study at night. I would help him by drilling him on the operating signals which included "Q" codes, "Z" codes, readability symbols, signal strength symbols, and prosigns; then there was the military lettering, phonetic alphabet, and the phonic sounds of international Morse code. Frank had to have all of these things memorized to complete his training at Fort Devens.

I loved the phonic sounds because they consisted of *di, dit,* and *dah* for letters in the alphabet. Just for fun, I learned these sounds then surprised Frank one evening by saying, "Di dit; di dah di dit, dah dah dah, di di di dah, dit; dah di dah dah, dah dah dah, di di dah," which means "I love you".

Frank had to make sure that his boots were always spit shined and his brass belt buckle shined, so while he did this at night, I made sure that his uniform was starched and pressed with the creases just in the right places. When I hand-washed these uniforms, they were rinsed then submerged in liquid starch before I hung them out to dry on the clothesline. After they were dry, I would iron them by sprinkling them with water as I ironed. Frank would wear his uniform for more than one day. so every night I would re-iron his uniform.

Now that our off-base allotment had started coming in, Frank and I decided on a Friday night that we would stuff all of our dirty clothes into his duffel bag and a couple of pillow-cases then get up early the next morning and walk into town to a laundromat. We thought it would be fun and we were pretty sure my "boogie clothes" system was not getting our clothes as clean as they could be.

It was Saturday morning but Frank and I got up early to start our walk into town to wash our clothes at the Laundro-mat. When we left the apartment Frank was carrying his Army duffel bag stuffed full of clothes, sheets, and towels. I was car-rying two pillowcases, one full of clothes and the other with detergent, bleach, and ammonia. We estimated that we were three miles from the laundromat that Frank's friend had told him about.

We were like two children on an adventure. Since I had only seen the town of Ayer a few times while riding in our friend's car as we drove through town on the way to and back from the commissary at Fort Devens, I was really excited about going to town.

Being Texans, Frank and I were waving at the vehicles we met on the road and saying hi to the people outside working in their yards. People were looking at us strangely but didn't wave back. Of course, this was around the time of the noto-rious Boston Strangler murders, so I am sure people were a little leery of unusual things and we probably looked strange carrying a big Army duffel bag stuffed tightly walking down the road. Frank and I didn't care we were having so much fun that we waved and shouted hi regardless.

When we reached the laundromat, I looked up to see the sign which made me laugh out loud: Bubble-It Laundromat. Frank and I walked in and then noticed the laundromat was full of people washing, drying and folding clothes. There was only one washing machine available, so we claimed it then decided to wash our white clothes first. Most of the people in the Laundromat seemed to know each other but were a little leery but friendly to us. The manager was at a table at the back of the large room and nodded to us then went back to what she was doing.

After we loaded all of the white clothes that would fit into the washer at one time, Frank and I added detergent and bleach but then decided that we should add some ammonia to the washer to help get those boogied clothes really clean. Frank and I closed the washer lid, started the washer, went to get a soda out of the vending machine in the laundromat then sat down to wait for the clothes to wash.

Oh, my goodness! When Frank and I looked towards the washing machine we were using and that dude was smoking! A cloud of vapor was rising from under the lid like a burning fire. People began to look in the direction of our washer and run out the front door of the Laundromat! Being young but not stupid, Frank and I ran out the door with them.

The manager of the laundromat, who was an older lady, was the last to exit through the door then walked directly over to us then said, "What did youse two put into that washing machine?"

We were both a little intimidated by her but Frank answered her question, "Clothes, detergent, bleach, and ammonia."

She looked at us like we were in some kinda deep trouble then threw her head back laughing saying, "Youse kids can't mix bleach and ammonia, together they make a toxic gas!"

Oops! Finally, the washer went to the rinse cycle and the washer mysteriously stopped smoking. The manager went into the laundromat, opened the windows, then after the laundromat aired out she told us all to come back inside.

The manager stayed by Frank and me for the rest of our time in the Laundromat. Maybe she had trust issues with us?

Frank and I actually splurged that afternoon and stopped at a little diner in Ayer where we bought the cheapest thing on the menu, sandwiches, then we started our walk back to our apartment.

Frank and I would return to the laundromat many more times in the future but we would only walk from our apartment out in the country to the laundromat then back that one time. It was a very special memorable time. We would laugh about this story many times through our life together and retell it to our family and friends.

A couple of weeks later we went for a drive with our friends. When we stopped at a filling station to get something to drink, the guys got out and went in to get the sodas while we girls stayed in the car.

When Frank came out of the store he had a big smile on his face then told me, "Nancy Lou, I just bought us a car."

I asked him, "What car?"

Frank just pointed to the parking lot on the side of the building. "Wow," was all I could say. This was not just any car! Red! This car was red and it had a little bit of white on the roof. Besides that, it had red leather seats with a red stirring wheel, big white wall tires and a long sleek body with what looked like fins in the back. The car was huge. Frank and I were running around looking at it, hugging each other, and acting like the two excited kids that we really were.

Our friends were very excited for us too. They told us to get in it, drive it, then they hugged us and left in their car.

We got the car started but then realized it did not have a shifter of any sort to put it in drive or reverse. Then we saw the push buttons on the dashboard. Frank and I both started laughing because we had never seen a push button shift car. "Big Fins" was not only red, but it had push buttons!

After we pulled out of the parking lot and got on the road, it occurred to me that I did not ask Frank how much he had paid for the car when I asked him he told me $35.⁰⁰. I couldn't believe it, we had gotten this car for a steal.

We drove out towards our apartment and on down the Sandy Pond Road towards the pond where the road had a bridge that crossed the pond at one of its narrow parts. When we started across the bridge a man standing on the bridge waved us down. Frank stopped the car and asked him what he wanted.

The man leaned in the window, looked at us sitting side by side then asked, "Are youse brother and sister?"

Frank answered him, "No, sir, we are husband and wife. Why would I let my sister sit this close to me? Why would you ask that?"

The man laughed then replied, "Youse guys look like brother and sister. Youse guys have to have a license tag to drive that car around."

Frank thanked him, then we turned the car around and headed back to our apartment. In our excitement, we had not noticed the car did not have license plates. We would have to check in to that on Monday because it was a Saturday evening. We decided to just sit in the car listening to the radio until dark then we went up to eat supper and went to bed.

The next morning we ate breakfast then ran out to see our car. When we got to the car we saw that to our amazement all four tires were flat. We could not afford to fix the tires, so now we were back to walking but we would spend evenings sitting in the car, listening to the radio, and talking about where we would drive it when we had the money to fix the tires.

Frank and I were making a few blunders but one thing for sure we were becoming one heart and soul with our love growing deeper and deeper.

25

apartment, snoopy, corn cob pipe

Frank had been searching for a new place for us to live in town. I was still surprised when he came home one afternoon saying he had found us a new home.

The new apartment was located on the third story of a brick building on Main Street in downtown Ayer, Massachusetts. The large building had offices on the second floor and a bank on the first floor. After entering the building through a big door in the middle of the building, a wide stairway led to the second-floor lobby which we walked through to get to another wide stairway that led to the third-floor landing where there were four apartments.

Our apartment was the only one with a back door. This door led to a fire escape with a small metal floored balcony that had metal stairs with metal hand railings on the sides which lead to the ground level. Mounted on the side of the building accessible from the balcony was a pulley system clothesline that was more than one hundred feet long with the other pulley mounted to a telephone pole. After figuring it out, I absolutely loved this pulley clothesline.

Also, Frank and I loved that we had another unique entrance way into our apartment with a small balcony to sit on at night and talk. Being three stories high up in the air also gave us a larger vision of things around us. Seems like we could see in the distance forever.

We only had three windows in the apartment. A very small window in the bathroom but there were two huge windows, one in the living room and one in the kitchen which had deep window seats. I loved to sit on those window seats and look out the windows.

We had to give up "Big Fins" because our previous apartment owner would not let us leave it parked there for a few days after we moved. Sadly, we had to get it towed away by a man who we signed it over to for the cost of the tow. Even now I remember that beautiful red and white car with the "big fins" and the memories of the dreams we shared with each other while sitting together in it.

Next door to our apartment building was a large grocery store where we could buy fresh vegetables, meat, and dairy products if we ran out during the month. Since we still did not have a car it saved us a taxi trip to the commissary on the base at Fort Devens.

Also, the Bubble It laundromat was only six blocks away and the lady who owned it did not seem to cringe every time we came in anymore after our smoking laundry incidence. This was a good thing since we only had a shower and no bathtub in our new bathroom. There would be no more "boogie clothes in this new apartment. You know what? I really did miss that!

Our best friends, who had helped us out so many times and made the best grilled cheese sandwiches ever, also moved into an apartment right down the hall from us. Frank and I were excited and thrilled to have them so close by.

Frank had met many people on base in his classes who were also married and, of course, single soldiers who were far from home. He would invite them over to eat, visit, and play cards which delighted me. Everyone would bring something with them to drink and eat. This way we all shared the expense of just playing cards and having fun.

Our new home would become the place where everyone liked to hang out, relax, and have fun on the weekends. We played many hands of double-decker pinochle, spades, and hearts. Lots of discussions about Vietnam, the Army, and the new "Age of Aquarius" went on around our kitchen table while we played cards. We were all young and knew a lot about nothing.

One of the wives of Frank's Army buddies was a bona-fide hippy flower child who hated the Army and he wanted to be an Army lifer. Still, to this very day, I wonder how their marriage worked out for them. She was so beautiful with long flowing hair and always had a flower pinned in her hair on one side of her head. She taught me how to make large flowers out of colored tissue paper and a pencil which I put in some clean empty pickle jars then sat them around the house for decoration.

Frank and I had moved into this new home the first part of September. Our birthdays were both in the first week of October. So, because it was his first birthday as me being his wife, I planned a surprise nineteenth birthday party for Frank.

Frank and I got up early on his nineteenth birthday because he had to go to school at Fort Devens that day. I fixed him a special breakfast then he was off to school.

Secretly I had plans for a surprise birthday party for him that evening. After he left for school, I started preparations for his party. First I cleaned the house then made him a unique cake. This was a homemade chocolate cake with chocolate icing which was shaped like a "Snoopy," Charlie Brown's pet beagle.

The reason for the shape of the cake did not really come from the comic strip but from a song that Frank and I always sang together called "Hang on Sloopy." When we sang the song we always changed Sloopy to Snoopy. We loved that song which was about a true love and not things.

To surprise Frank, I had asked his best friend to come over and take him for an outing right after they got home from the base that afternoon knowing that it would give me time to set up for the surprise party. When Frank got home from school he changed out of his uniform, then just as planned his friend knocked on our door and asked him to go on an errand with him.

After they left my best friend, the wife of friend Frank had just left on an errand with, came over to help me set up the table and do decorations. Once we were through we waited for other friends to arrive.

All of the guests arrived then we all went into the living room, sat down, and waited to surprise Frank. Needless to say, an hour passed but Frank and his buddy had not returned then we all heard a loud commotion coming up the stairs to our apartment landing. Frank was singing loudly and laughing when he opened our front door as we all yelled surprise.

Frank was smiling with his big ole dimples, smoking a corncob pipe, and quite drunk but his buddy just stood behind him laughing. Everyone in the room started laughing but we were all in for a much bigger laugh when I lit the candles on the cake and put a birthday hat on Frank's head.

As we all sang "Happy Birthday," Frank leaned down, took a huge bite out of his Snoopy cake getting chocolate icing all over his shirt! Of course, I took a picture!

The rest of the evening was fairly quiet as we all returned to the living room to visit. Frank would eventually pass out on the small couch while telling us all about him and his friend's afternoon adventures.

Two days later Frank would surprise me with a dozen red roses for my birthday and cook me a fabulous supper.

Our new home was the beginning of many new adventures for the two of us.

26

turn off the water?

ince we had moved to town, life had become less stress-
ful for Frank and me. Our apartment rent was $25.^{00}
cheaper, which gave us more money to spend on food.
We still didn't have a car, a phone, air-conditioning, washer,
dryer, or a television but we thanked God every day for the
extra food on our table and each other.

When Frank got home in the evenings we had supper
then we would take long walks on the sidewalks of downtown
Ayer, looking in the windows of all the stores, or we would
just sit on our fire escape balcony watching the stars come out
at night.

My days were full of cleaning and cooking from the
Betty Crocker Cookbook that we had received as a wedding
gift. I really loved to cook. After all, I was in homemaking
in high school for two years with a teacher that taught us to
make all kinds of goodies.

Frank loved that I liked to cook and surprise him with
cookies, cakes, pies, and homemade bread.

After Frank left for work, I made the bed, picked up
around the house, and washed the dishes then I decided to do
something about the floor in the kitchen. Our kitchen floor
was linoleum mostly a white color with scattered pieces of
black lines in it. It was really worn and needed a really good
scrubbing.

I decided the best way to get it clean was to get down on
my hands and knees with a bucket of warm soapy water and
a scrub brush. The kitchen in our new apartment was really
large, so I decided to scrub the floor one section at a time
working towards the back door.

All of this scrubbing then changing the bucket full of
soapy water while rinsing the floor took quite awhile. The
back door was wide open to help dry the floor, so once getting

to the door, I stepped out on to the fire escape patio then set down for a while dangling my feet off of the patio.

It was a beautiful October day with the trees beginning to turn into Fall colors. After sitting there a while taking in the beauty around me, I decided that the floor had to be dry, so I went back inside to the kitchen. After looking at the clock, I decided it was time to start cooking supper.

Frank would be coming in from school soon in about an hour. I made meatloaf which went into the oven to cook for a while as I made some white rice which was Frank's favorite dish. Another look at the clock told me that I just had time to take a shower before Frank got home.

After closing the back door and locking it, I also locked the front door that led to the landing to the apartments then I went into the bathroom for a shower. Our bathroom was off of the kitchen. The door to the bathroom was actually on the same wall as our front door and the two doors were only separated by about five feet of wall.

The warm water of the shower felt so wonderful that I held my head under the water for a long time just letting the water run down my back which felt so good. Out of nowhere, there was a banging noise. I opened the shower curtain slightly then stuck my head out when I heard the banging louder along with a man shouting at the bathroom door, "Shut the water off!" over and over again while banging loudly on the door.

Even though terrified, I grabbed the bathrobe hanging on a hook by the shower, put it on quickly and only then turned off the shower. Dripping wet in the bathrobe, I mustered up enough courage then went to the bathroom door.

Suddenly, I heard Frank's voice saying, "What are you doing in my house?"

I opened the door, stepped out of the bathroom into the kitchen and stood there trying not to shake. Evidently, the banging intruder was our landlord. He was ranting, raving, and waving his arms at Frank about a water leak from our shower to the floors below.

Frank looked at me standing there water dripping from my hair, shaking, and probably pale as a ghost then turned back to face the landlord who was still shouting at the top of his lungs.

Frank asked him, "How did you get into my house?"

I had never seen Frank's face so intense and serious. Each word he spoke was spoken very deliberately one at a time.

The landlord yelled back, "When no one answered the damn front door, I used my key to open it then went to the bathroom door, and banged on it to get her (he then pointed to me) to turn the damn shower off!"

Frank's face turn red while he stared at the man then again with each word spoken deliberately one at a time very he said, "You opened my front door with your key, entered my house while my wife was in the shower, and banged on the bathroom door?"

The landlord yelled back at Frank, "Yes, I did!"

Before I could say a word or move, Frank lifted the man up by the front of his shirt then slammed him into the wall holding the man there with his feet dangling off the floor. Frank drew back his fist and was fixing to hit the man when I grabbed his fisted arm asking him to please not hit him.

Frank looked at my face and immediately his features softened then told the landlord, "This is our home. Nobody enters our home without our permission. Ever. Nancy is my wife and nobody is allowed to scare her or harm her in any way or I will personally make them wish they were dead. Damn you, my wife was in the shower! Never come into this house again while we live here!"

Frank let go of the terrified landlord and who slid down the wall until his feet touched the floor. Frank asked him one more question, "Did you ever think about just shutting the water off?"

The landlord did not answer as he went through the front door quickly and closed it behind him. Frank turned to look at me then pulled me into his arms. I was still shaking but the tears running down my face were not from fear anymore but because of the love in my heart for the beautiful man who was holding me close, wiping away my tears, kissing my face, and telling me how much he loved me.

Frank held me for a long time while stroking my wet hair telling me that he would always protect me from harm. Finally, I quit shaking then went into the bedroom and got dressed. When I returned to the kitchen Frank was busy getting our supper on to plates so we could eat.

We ate supper, washed the dishes together, then went out onto our small balcony. We sat there for a long time dangling our feet off of the side, holding each other, talking quietly, being in love, and watching the stars come out brightly.

I am not sure what I would have done that day if Frank had not come home at the moment he did but I do know God had his hands all over the situation.

From that day on, I have never feared anything or anyone no matter what life has thrown my way. Being loved by God and Frank with love that has transcended through the dimensions of all space and time have been eternal blessings and the greatest blessings God could have ever given me.

27

texas & the plastic fab. co.

Frank and I were trying to save as much money as we could, knowing in a couple of months when Frank's school ended that it would be time for us to leave Ayer, Massachusetts. We knew extra money would be needed to ship our things home. Frank could fly military stand-by free, but the extra money would also be needed to buy my student stand-by airline ticket. We were really hoping to get to fly together when we left for home.

One Friday afternoon, my best friend came over to our house and told us that there was a job opening at the Union Products Inc., which was a plastic fabrication company in Leominster, Massachusetts but the factory was actually located in Fitchburg. Since she worked there in their office, she wanted to let us know first and see if I would like to go to work. I was really excited about the thought of getting a job, knowing it would help us out with having enough money to ship our things and buy my ticket home but Frank shook his head from side to side then told her, "No."

I was speechless and puzzled by his response but didn't say anything. My friend told him that I could ride back and forth to work with her to work and I would be safe. Frank told her that he and I would discuss it that night then get back with her the next day.

Of course, after my friend left so did my speechlessness. I asked Frank, "Why did you say no? I want to work and we actually could use the money."

Frank saw the excitement in my face then he smiled at me while answering my question with, "Nancy, I should be able to take care of you without you working. I can't protect you if you are working in that factory. It's twenty miles away and we don't have a car. What if something happens to you?"

Knowing that Frank was smiling when he answered me, I knew that there was a yes inside him if I could think of the right thing to say or do to convince him.

After walking over to Frank then hugging him tightly, I told him, "Frank, I will be there with my best friend, she knows how to get in touch with you on the base, and she has a car. So, there is no reason for me not to go to work. It's gonna be so much fun and thanks for letting me do this."

Shaking his head while he smiled, Frank said, "Okay, Nancy, I can't tell you no but you have to promise me you will be careful."

Of course, I promised him then quickly ran to our friend's apartment and told her that Frank said yes!

Monday morning early, my friend and I set out for Union Products Inc. in Fitchburg. I was nervous but she assured me that the job was mine because she had already told her boss all about me.

When my friend and I arrived at the factory, we went into the manager's office and she introduced me to him then he handed me some paperwork to fill out. After finishing filling out the paperwork, I handed it back to him. Without even looking at the paperwork, he told me I was hired.

Trying not to scream out loud from the excitement inside of me, I thanked him then he told me to follow him. All of the workers were snacking on their breakfast in the lunchroom when the manager led me into that large room. He introduced me to the workers then asked me to tell everyone a little about myself which I did.

All of the workers seemed to be sitting on the edge of their chairs waiting for me to finish each word spoken. When I finished talking, they all burst out laughing and for some reason, I laughed with them.

Not sure if you know this, people from the New England states talk really fast. Evidently, my drawn-out Texas drawl was really funny to them but I laughed with them because they spoke so quickly that I couldn't understand a word they said and had to keep asking them to repeat themselves.

A loud "ringer noise thangy" went off then the workers all started walking towards the inside of the factory. The manager told me to follow him then we walked into another large room which had two long conveyor belts, one on each side of the room.

When we got to the end of one conveyor belt, the manager told me that was where I would be working. He said that I would take the flatten cardboard boxes, open them up, fold the two short flaps on one end towards the center of the box, then fold the long flaps of the boxes over them towards the center, and tape the long flaps down. This would make the box ready to put merchandise into it.

Next, he showed me the tape machine "thangy." It dispensed the tape which was made of paper, prepasted like an envelope, and the same color as the boxes. At the end of the tape machine, was another dumaflotce that actually wet the glue on the tape, and a sharp cutter that cut the tape a certain length.

The manager showed me how to make one of the boxes then let me make a box. He told me that I would be putting the different pieces of merchandise which would be assembled then grouped by other workers into the premade boxes I had made as it came down the conveyor belt then seal the tops of the boxes exactly the way we had done the bottom of the box.

As he walked away, the manager told me to make some more boxes, which he stopped a minute and watched me make, then asked me if I thought I was ready for the conveyor to start running. Thinking, you betcha as I told him, "Yes, sir." The manager left my side as I continued to make boxes then the conveyor belt started to move. The plastic table top Christmas trees and their prepackaged parts seemed to be spaced out fairly well and for about five minutes I kept up really great until the conveyor belt picked up speed.

Oh my goodness! I was running to the belt putting stuff in the boxes, trying to tape them closed, and then the conveyor belt stopped. Everyone in the room had gathered around me then started to laugh. Seems they thought it was funny to break in the new girl.

The manager had sped up the conveyor belt just for fun. Actually, he told me, my job was just to make and close the boxes which had nothing to do with the conveyor belt. Then the manager told me. "Texas, you did pretty well for a slow talker. I think we will just have to keep youse around for a while."

From that moment on everyone called me "Texas."

I worked hard the rest of the day and couldn't wait to get home to tell Frank all about my day. When I got home that evening, Frank was already home cooking supper when he met me at the door and I blurted out all that happened at work. We laughed together for a long time then while he finished cooking supper, I took a shower.

When we sat down to eat when Frank noticed that my hands had paper cuts all over them from the paper tape. He asked me if the cuts hurt but I told him no. Of course, the cuts hurt and my hands were sore but I didn't want Frank to know that. I wasn't some kind of sissy or quitter.

After we finished eating, Frank told me he was going to run downstairs to the grocery store. When he got back he had a bottle of Corn Huskers lotion which he applied to my hands. It burnt like all get out but it sealed the cuts and made them quit hurting. Corn Huskers lotion became my best friend when I got home from work at night for nearly a month then I was moved to a different position at the factory.

My next job was heat-treating the three-foot plastic Santas with a blow torch which made the paint stick when the painters spray painted them. I really loved this job even though I burnt my arm once with the blowtorch while heat-treating a Santa Claus. I guess Santa didn't like the heat. Of course, Frank doctored it with Foile burn cream and wrapped with some gauze after I got home while giving me a lecture on being safe and careful.

Everyone took their lunch to work and we all ate in the lunch room together. After we had eaten the rest of lunchtime I spent answering questions about cowboys (girls), Indians, horses, and big ranches which always seemed to have everyone sitting on the edge of their seats wishing I could talk faster then asking me what "thangy" meant.

Seems everyone at the factory thought everyone in Texas had a big ranch, was a cowboy (girl) who wore ten-gallon hats and chased Indians while riding horses. Of course, I let them think some of that was really true.

I learned to like ice coffee which they sold in the vending machine at the factory. It actually looked like milk with a little coffee and sugar in it. It was a wonderful experience working at the factory.

I met lots of good hardworking people of all ages who were just ordinary people trying to make a living. I was sad when the time came for me to leave but I had found out something about myself which was that I could learn how to do anything.

Looking at my last check stub I found from November 22, 1968, it says I made $51.[20] for thirty-two hours work which means I made $1.^{60} an hour. Thinking that was not to bad for my very first real job.

Frank and I were getting ever closer and we were handling everything by trial an error but God was taking care of us.

28

rope knot & bivouac

We were really having an awesome time just being together. Our love was growing deeper and deeper with each passing day. God had wrapped us in His loving arms protecting us with a love for us that was so evident. We felt Him surround us every day. He had given us, the greatest gift, true love for each other. Looking back, I really believe that God had planned our love from our births and He was delighted by the way we loved each other and loved watching us grow up together.

We had made many new close friends and we were finally more secure financially. Now, we had money for food with a little extra to put in a savings account which we would need to get our things shipped home then buy my airline ticket home.

Early December 1968, Frank was also told that he would go on bivouac for a week at Fort Devens and he received his orders for transfer to his next assignment and that would be at Torii Station in Okinawa. Okinawa was one of the Ryukyu Islands in the Pacific Ocean, which had been a territory of the United States since WWII. Frank would also receive a thirty-day leave after he finished the bivouac training to go home to visit our families before he flew to Okinawa.

With a heavy heart, I gave notice to the manager at the factory where I worked. It was a sweet goodbye to the wonderful people that I had worked with but they all wished Frank and Texas many blessings in our future travels. When I left work that last day there were a lot of tears.

While Frank was out on bivouac I packed all of our things into the two huge barrels that we had shipped them into Ayer, Massachusetts. This would prove to be an adventurous week and with another fun story to tell.

Frank had to go on a little camping trip called bivouac at Fort Devens for a week of the last ten days that we lived in Ayer, Massachusetts. Before Frank left he instructed me over and over with things that he did not want me to do while he was gone.

"Don't go outside after dark. Don't open the door to anybody whose voice you do not recognize. Don't lift heavy stuff or hurt yourself. Keep the doors closed and locked. Don't tell anyone I am away on bivouac. Don't talk to the landlord. Ever!"

Frank was such a worry-wart.

Well, I knew that his last "don't" would be very easy for me because I would never talk to the landlord but the others were iffy. I promised Frank that all would be great and that I had lots of packing to do to keep me out of trouble. Frank smiled as he told me he loved me, hugged me tightly then kissed me at the door. I closed and locked the door then as I walked away, I heard a knock at the door. I opened the door and there stood Frank smiling then he asked, "Did you ask who was at the door when I knocked?"

I started laughing then told him, "No, I didn't ask who was at the door because I knew you would came back for one more kiss."

Frank rolled his eyes at me and smiled showing his amazing dimples then said, "Nancy Lou, you need to do what I told you."

Frank kissed me again but, of course, to not be outdone I asked him, " I need to know something, are you gonna knock on the door again after I close it because if you are, I won't have to ask who is there?"

Laughing Frank said, "Only if I decide to come back to give you a spanking, Nancy Lou!"

He kissed me again then closed the door but as I locked the door I heard him say from the other side of the door, "I love you, Nancy," then he quickly walked away and down the stairs.

Suddenly the room felt very empty and lonely. I stood there a few moments staring at the door and missing him already. Realizing I had lots to do which would make the time pass quicker, so I got busy taking things out of the cabinets to start wrapping them up with towels or paper to pack them into the barrels.

The day after Frank left for bivouac it started to snow in Ayer, Massachusetts. The snow was absolutely beautiful, so I bundled up in some warm clothing then went out the back door, down the fire escape, to walk in the snow. Having lived in the Panhandle of Texas from age two until twelve, I had played in lots of snow. After spending about thirty minutes outside walking around while it snowed and holding my head back letting snowflakes fall on my tongue, I decided to go back up the stairs to the apartment.

I pulled the door to close it behind me because as a door that went to a fire escape it swung open to the outside. Evidently, I must have pulled it a little harder than normal since the doorknob broke, came off in my hand, and the knob on the other side of the door fell on to the balcony. I picked it up then brought both doorknobs inside the kitchen.

Dagnabit! All I could think of as I looked at that doorknob was one of Frank's "Don'ts" which was, "Don't talk to the Landlord!" After examining the doorknobs, I could tell that the doorknobs could not be fixed. The one doorknob didn't just come off in my hand but the rod had broken which went through the door that they attached to.

It was getting dark outside, so I had to decide how to fix the door to keep it closed and secure. I found some rope that Frank and his buddy had used to tie down one of the barrels to the top of his buddy's car when we moved to town.

After putting one end of the rope through the hole in the door from the inside, I brought it around to the inside passing the doorframe then placed it into my hand which held the other end of the rope. Next, I pulled the door closed squeezing the rope between the door and the doorframe until it was shut tightly then I tied knot after knot tightly against closed door and doorframe.

I stepped back and decided that nobody could get into the apartment but then noticed that there was still a hole that the doorknob had covered which light would shine through, so I decided to take some "fawl" (Texan for *foil*) and stuff the hole with it then I smiled thinking how the problem had been solved. Of course, I would not be able to use the back door but I didn't care. Later, I pulled the mattress off of the bed then into the kitchen and slept next to the back door just as an extra precaution.

Finally, the days passed, our things were all packed in the barrels, but most importantly, Frank came home. He looked very tired and had a nasty cold. I asked him what had happened out there on bivouac and when he told me I wanted to scream. Seems that they were playing a few war games with objectives to accomplish certain things without getting caught by the people declared as the enemy.

Okay, that was fine with me but it seems the "enemy" included some drunk "tramp" officer's wives who got to do the interrogations which included stuffing snow down the front of the captured soldier's pants, sticking two wires in the snow which were attached to a hand crank generator, then cranked the dang thang until the soldier talked. I was so mad that I couldn't breathe. No other woman was allowed to touch my husband like that, ever. Nancy Lou was seeing red and not a happy camper.

After catching my breath, I asked Frank if he got caught. Frank told me that after the first soldier got caught they released him back to their base camp when the word spread of what had happened to him, they all decided that they were not going to get caught whatever it took. Frank spent one night covered under snow in a shallow stream after hearing the enemy getting close but he said they finally overtook the enemy and achieved their objectives.

While Frank took a hot shower, I fixed him some warm soup and stewed a little bit myself about those bivouac tramps. After he ate, I tucked him into bed then laid down beside him hugging him tightly to keep him warm until he fell asleep. I didn't fall to sleep right away because my mind wouldn't let me quit thinking about those drunk bivouac tramps.

The next morning, Frank asked me about the back door with the rope tied through it. I told him what had happened and he started laughing then he walked over to the door, pushed on it, and it opened wide up. I had this shocked look on my face as Frank started laughing and told me, "Nancy Lou, I think you needed more knots in that rope."

I followed most of the "Don'ts" that Frank told me, of course, I told you some might be "iffy." One thing that would never be "iffy" was the love we had so deep in our hearts and souls for each other.

29

going back home

A fter Frank got home from bivouac, we still had a few things to do. We had to take the fully packed barrels with all of our things packed in them to be shipped through REA Express. This company could ship by truck, plane, ship, or train. Our things were shipped, by train from Ayer, Massachusetts to Bay City, Texas.

Since we had to be out of our apartment in town on December 15, 1968, Frank and I had to find a place to stay for a few days before we left Ayer, Massachusetts. Our friends had already moved back to Iowa, so we could not stay with them. Frank would not be through at Fort Devens until December 18, 1968, so he rented us a room at the NCO Guest Housing on base for five days which cost us $3.^{00} a day for a grand total of $15.^{00}.

The room was small with two twin beds that had a small nightstand separating them. We had a community bathroom down the hall from our room, which was small but convenient. It had been snowing for about a week or two and the base looked like a Winter Wonderland. The snow reflected the Christmas lights at night that were hung up all over Fort Devens.

While Frank was finishing his transfer paperwork during the day while we were staying at the guest housing, I walked around on the base close to the unit we were staying in. Frank actually finished up quicker than we expected so we had some days to just hang out on the base together.

The last night we were on the base, December 18, 1968, we took a long walk together in the new snow that had fallen during the day carrying our faithful battery-powered transistor radio. We decided to walk off the base a couple of miles to a diner in Ayer where we ate a hamburger then had a piece of hot apple pie with cheese ala mode. This was the first time I had ever eaten apple pie with melted cheese and ice cream on it. It was awesome.

After we ate we decided to walk down the main street of Ayer past our apartment building one more time as we tried to soak in all of the memories of living there into our minds. As we walked hand in hand down a back road to get back to the base we came to a bridge that crossed a stream. The bridge was covered in snow but had not been crossed by vehicles, animals or other people on foot, so we were the first to get to leave our footprints in the freshly fallen snow hoping they would stay there forever.

Frank and I stopped in the middle of the bridge, set the transistor radio down on one side of the railing of the bridge, then we kissed as new snowflakes fell from the sky. As if by some sort of humorous magic, the transistor radio started playing a song by Blue Suede, "Hooked on a Feeling." Frank and I started laughing and singing together as we walked hand in hand back to the base knowing that we were both hooked on that feeling.

The next morning, December 19, 1968, Frank and I took a cab to Boston, Massachusetts. Frank had decided that we should spend the night in Boston because our plane would leave very early the next morning. We rented a room in a hotel which was downtown. That afternoon, we walked to an indoor picture show bought tickets, went in, and watched a movie. When the movie was over we walked to what was called the Boston Common, a park in central Boston. It was a beautiful park and there were many people in the park of all ages playing in the snow, throwing snowballs, and just having fun. We sat on a bench in the park and watched for a long time then we went back to the hotel for supper.

Early the next morning Frank and I took a cab to the Airport. I really think that might have been the wildest ride I have ever taken in a vehicle. When we got to a tunnel opening, six lanes were converging into two lanes and our cab driver got so close to sideswiping other cars as he honked the horn trying to push his way through the other vehicles that I couldn't even watch, of course, Frank thought it was hilarious.

Finally, we arrived at the Airport then went inside to check in. Frank had made sure that we would be flying in the same plane, in seats next to each other for the entire trip to Texas. We would only change planes in New York at Kennedy Airport then it was a "straight" nonstop flight to Hobby Airport in Houston, Texas. We had never flown together and we were both excited about getting to do that.

Our flight to New York Kennedy Airport went great but we only had a short layover so we only saw what we could see of New York from the airport windows. Once we boarded the airplane which would take us to Houston, we got settled in because we knew that flight would be a little longer than our last one. The airplane was absolutely loaded with passengers. It was five days until Christmas and everyone was in a joyful mood.

After the plane took off the stewardesses made sure everyone had something to drink and munch on but then we started hitting major turbulence as the "fasten your seatbelt" lights came on. The pilot of the plane came on the loudspeaker then told us that there was a major winter storm coming into the East Coast and our flight would have to take a different route. He explained to us that this route would take us out over the Atlantic Ocean until he could veer the plane more directly towards Texas.

ThepPilot of the plane could have just stopped right there with his explanation but either he had been drinking too much eggnog or he had a strange sense of humor as he went on to tell us how many miles we had left to fly, how many miles the plane could go on a gallon of aviation fuel, and how many gallons of fuel the plane had left at that moment. Of course, I am pulling out a pen and paper from my purse trying to figure it all out when the pilot came back on the speaker telling us, "If you are a praying person, pray!"

The whole plane got really quiet as we bounced up and down from the turbulence. I know I squeezed Frank's hand until it had no circulation but Frank kept telling me, "I love you, Nancy. It is Christmastime and God isn't gonna let us miss our first Christmas together."

I looked at him then told him how much I loved him then managed to give him a big smile. The flight seemed to go on forever but finally, the pilot came on the loudspeaker again then said, "Hallelujah! Must be some good praying people back there, because I see Hobby Airport coming up in the distance! Thank you for your prayers!"

All the passengers started clapping and cheering including the two of us then I released Frank's hand. Frank told me he was glad that the flight wasn't longer because he absolutely thought he would never be able to get circulation back in his hand. Of course, he laughed. We landed safely then couldn't wait to get off of that plane. Our parents and siblings were all in the terminal to greet us as we came down the ramp into the terminal. Everyone was so excited and there were lots of hugs and kisses.

Frank and I decided to ride to Van Vleck with our folks in separate cars. I rode with my folks and Frank rode with his folks. After we reached Van Vleck each of us visited with our folks at their different houses. Well, this was all fine and dandy until it was bedtime and we realized we were three miles apart without a car.

My folk's phone rang about midnight and it was Frank. He asked to speak to me then his exact words were, "Nancy

Lou, either I come there are you come here. Either way is fine with me but I am not sleeping without you by my side."

Of course, I totally agreed with him. Frank borrowed his Dad's car then came to my folk's home for the night. We would trade out staying at one house or the other during the thirty days before Frank left for Okinawa but we would never spend a night apart.

Frank and I were in Ayer, Massachusetts together from June 1, 1968, until December 20, 1968. In those six and a half months we had become totally reliant on each other and our love for each other had taken us to such a deep place of being one heart and soul. We were definitely "hooked on a feeling."

30

next stop: okinawa

A fter arriving home in Texas late in the evening of December 20, 1968, Frank and I had only a few days to shop for gifts for our families before Christmas. Since Frank's car had been left at his folk's house while we were in Ayer, Massachusetts, we actually had a car we could drive into Bay City or Houston to shop.

Frank's little sister, Cindy, was not yet two-years-old, so there was a lot of excitement going on with that little one in Frank's folk's home. She really loved her big brother and he absolutely adored her. As a matter of fact, they looked so much alike that when we were out in stores with her in tow, people actually thought she was our little girl.

Our first Christmas together was awesome. We spent a lot of time visiting with everyone and eating the most awesome food. The New Year was ushered in and we all celebrated together but with the new year came the realization that Frank was running out of leave time and would soon depart for Okinawa leaving me behind in Texas for a while.

Mid-January 1969, Frank, his family, and I would travel to Hobby Airport in Houston, Texas to say good-bye before Frank loaded onto an airplane to fly to Okinawa. After telling Frank how much I loved him, hugging him and then kissing him before he loaded the plane, I stood at the window and watched as his plane took off. Tears ran down my face but strength came to my heart as I realized that I would do all in my power to get to Okinawa to be by his side again as soon as possible.

I needed a passport, lots of shots, and a job to make money for my ticket to Okinawa, which would cost at least $600. Frank would be working to getting approval for me to go to Okinawa and get lots of paperwork done through his superiors on the base for us to live in off-base housing and then permission for me to get a visa to live in Okinawa.

Frank and I could talk through shortwave radio operators. This was an interesting way of talking on the phone. When he wanted to talk to me, Frank would go to the base radio operators then they would try to reach an operator closest to Van Vleck, Texas then the operator would make a collect call to my folk's or Frank's folk"s home.

When the phone was answered, the fun really started. Every statement or question was followed by "Over" then the other end of the line got to answer your question or make a statement followed by "Over." Of course, this was never a private conversation due to the operators listening in and the party lines in Van Vleck, Texas but it was real voice communication. I always hated the "Out" part, which meant the conversation had ended and the call was done.

After getting my passport done, ten thousand shots and a physical at Ellington Air Force Base in Houston, I applied for and was hired as a grocery store checker at H.E.B. in Bay City, Texas. I would reach into the grocery basket, grab an item, and key the price in manually on the cash register because of the price of each item, which was stamped on it in ink. There were no scan tags on the grocery items. Then I would bag the groceries myself in brown paper bags.

Each day I arrived early to look over a table full of different grocery items that had been placed at the front of the store which would be on sale that day because I had to memorize the sale price of them. The grocery items could not be scanned so price changes were our responsibility as checkers through memorization.

Actually, this whole process was fun and the checkers all challenged each other to see who could check out the largest number of people in a day. On a busy payday Saturday, I worked from opening to closing (twelve hours, including two breaks and a thirty-minute lunch) checking out 243 people and my end cash register money total was exactly correct.

I was so proud of that particular accomplishment that I told Frank all about in our next long distance "Over" conversation.

Oh, I forgot to mention, we had to know how to make correct change, there was not a machine telling us how much change to give the customer back. Also if our register money came out short, you were responsible, and the shortage came out of your paycheck.

Finally, on April 9, 1969, eighty days after Frank left for Okinawa, I boarded a plane at Hobby Airport in Houston, Texas.

After arriving at Hobby Airport, I said good-byes to all of my family and friends that had gone to wish me a safe journey to Okinawa then I loaded on to the airplane. My Uncle Billy, my dad's brother, was an air traffic controller at Hobby Airport and once everyone had loaded, the pilot of the airplane came on the loudspeaker saying, "Ladies and gentlemen, today we have a Nancy Blakley Henderson on board and her Uncle Billy wishes her a *bon voyage* and a safe trip."

I was totally surprised and happy that my Uncle would be helping with the take-off of the airplane but not as surprised as when the stewardess came toward my seat with my daddy following her. Daddy had told her that he had forgotten to see if I needed some extra money but I knew that daddy knew it would be two years before he would see me again. He just needed to hug his only daughter one more time and say a private goodbye. I was nineteen and married but I would always be my daddy's "Sugar."

As the plane took off, I was not afraid at all because soon there would be a wonderful reunion with the love of my life at the end of my journey. I could not wait to see Frank, hold him, and kiss him. The two weeks we were separated before I had arrived at Ayer, Massachusetts, were nothing compared to the eighty days we had then been apart.

The plane landed at Seattle Washington Airport where there would be a short layover before my boarding a plane to Japan. There were four other women in the waiting room, so I sat down by them. A soldier came into the waiting room then sat down not two seats from me. He looked familiar but I couldn't place where I might have seen him. He kept watching me which made me uncomfortable, so I decided to start up a conversation with one of the women sitting beside me. All of the women were going to Okinawa to live with their husbands and would also, like me, be spending the night in Japan before flying to Okinawa the next morning. I was so happy to have company for my entire trip to Okinawa.

Finally, my flight number was called over the loudspeaker and we were asked to load an airplane. All of the women I had been sitting with loaded the airplane with me. After we all set down then one male soldier, after another male soldier, after another male soldier loaded the plane until it was absolutely full. The four women and I had been put on a military flight to Japan. Evidently, I had paid $600 for a seat on a military flight. The other women who were going to Okinawa to be with their husbands must have been traveling for free by military flights. Why I was on board that plane was anyone's guess but I certainly wasn't going to get off. The plane had seats on both sides, each row had three seats.

One of the women sat down near a window then I sat down in the middle seat next to her. We were talking when I heard a male voice asked me, "Ma'am, may I sit in this seat?"

When I turned to see who it was, it was the soldier who had been watching me in the waiting room. Not knowing what to do, I told him sure but in my mind, wanted to say no.

He sat down then said, "I don't mean to scare you. I flew out of Hobby Airport on the same plane that you did. Your dad approached me before I loaded that plane, asked where I was headed, and asked if I would look out for you until we part ways in Japan."

Instantly, I started to relax. We were told to buckle our seatbelts by a male steward then I noticed that we had all male stewards, which was strange and the first time I had ever witnessed it. Evidently, unless the pilot was female, there were only five women on the flight.

Once we were in the air, the stewards started taking drink orders. Of course, I ordered a coke, but it seems the rest of the plane except for the three in my row of seats were drinking straight liquor. It didn't take long for the plane to get loud and rowdy. I asked the soldier next to me where he was going and he told me to Korea then told me that all of the other soldiers on the flight were headed there too. I told him where I was going, all about Frank then showed him Frank's picture.

After we flew over the International Dateline, the stewards were handing out large amounts of booze by the bottles. I could hear some of the women in the back of the plane laughing loudly, giggling and definitely drunk. Sounded like they were being really loyal and faithful to their husbands.

As I was talking to the soldier beside me about Frank, a soldier in the seat in front of me turn around to face us. He was obviously drunk when he said, "You know your husband is screwing around on you, don't you? Lots of bars and hookers in Okinawa."

Before I could say anything the soldier sitting next to me punched him in the face, then the whole plane erupted into some kind of drunk mayhem. People started yelling "Fight! Fight! Fight!" The soldier next to me grabbed the other soldier by the throat and told him to apologize to me but instead, the guy went to swinging.

Terror and fright hit me! I was so afraid they would make the plane crash! Tears streamed down my face as I stood up then shouted at the top of my lungs, "Please stop! You are scaring me! I have to get to my husband!"

For some reason the plane suddenly got quiet. I stood there and stared into the face of the drunk soldier who had been sitting in front of me. As blood trickled from his nose, I told him, "My husband doesn't cheat on me, he loves me, and if you ever speak to me again this Texas girl will slap your face so hard that your buddies will see you cry. You just don't mess with Frank's wife."

Then I sat back down in my seat. The soldier who was sitting next to me sat back down too then he told me he was sorry he had scared me. I told him, "No, thank you for taking up for another soldiers wife. I will tell Frank your name and all about what you did for me."

We made it to Japan just as the sunset, just like it had been doing the whole trip. After going through customs the women and I were taxied by bus to a hotel where we would spend the night. The next morning we were taxied back to the airport then we loaded a small plane which flew us the short trip to Okinawa.

When we unloaded the plane in Okinawa, I could see the owner of my heart standing in the crowd. My heart was pounding so hard that I could barely breathe as I rushed into his arms. Frank hugged me, kissed me, and told me how much he loved me, then I cried because I knew that we were now complete again.

31

settling in

Ｗe left Naha Airport hand in hand with big smiles on our faces. Frank and I were back together again, nothing else in the world mattered at that moment.

It was still early in the day, so we took a cab to Kadena Circle then turned off on a road then in just a couple of blocks, we were at the house that Frank had rented for us to live in.

After leaving my suitcase in the house, we decided to walk to a town not far from our house called Kadena.

We walked around looking in the open front stores then we went to a restaurant which was approved with a three A rating above the door at the entry. Frank told me about a dish that was made at the restaurant, called Yakisoba, it was a mixture of noodles, shredded vegetables, and chicken that you put soy sauce on. I totally loved it which made Frank very happy.

After finishing eating, we walked back to our new home. Our household things which had been shipped from Texas would not arrive for weeks because they were coming by ship but Frank had purchased basic kitchen utensils, sheets, towels, a refrigerator, a small three burner electric stove, and a bed.

The refrigerator had cheeses, apples, and milk in it but the counter next to it had crackers, black olives, pickles, and crackers of all kinds. Next to the food on the counter was a large bottle of champagne with two glasses next to it. Frank had carefully planned our reunion to be a very special occasion and it was more than special, it was amazing.

The next morning, I woke to the smell of fresh coffee then Frank entered the bedroom with two cups of coffee. We planned our day as we drank our morning coffee sitting side by side on the bed.

We had lots to do which included going to the GRI. (Government of the Ryukyuan Islands) Immigration to get a residence visa which would let me stay longer than thirty days in Okinawa, one of the Ryukyuan Islands.

Frank had all of the paperwork that we needed from the Army and I had my passport plus extra pictures. We took a bus to Naha where the Immigration Office was located and it did not take very long to apply for the issuance of my residence certificate. Frank had done all of the homework ahead of time. One thing for sure, he was not going to let them take me from his arms. (Did I tell you how much love this man?)

After leaving the Immigration Office, we walked the streets of Naha. It was a busy small city with so many shops which all had open front shops. So many beautiful oriental furniture, knickknacks, and all kinds of interesting foods. We spent hours enjoying the wonder of it all then we took the bus back to our new home.

The third morning Frank and I got up early, got dressed then ate breakfast. We decided the night before that we needed some more furniture since all we had was a bed. We also needed curtains since we had only sheets on the bedroom windows and had to make a mad dash to the bathroom if not fully dressed. There was a clothesline in our backyard but we did not have a washing machine, so we decided to get a used washing machine too.

We came home owning two chairs, a loveseat-size couch, curtains, and, most importantly, a washing machine. The used washing machine cost us $15.^{00} and it actually worked! The Okinawan store owners delivered our furniture and washing machine to our home as soon as we arrived back at the house. I could not wait to get started hanging the curtains, so I did that immediately Frank and I still had snack food, so we decided to just eat what we had instead of taking a cab to the base to shop in the commissary.

Day four was an early day too but we really needed food, so off to the commissary at Kadena Air Force Base we went. We had to take a cab to the base but then we had to switch into another cab at the gate. Only certain cabs were allowed on the base and they were parked inside the gate. After buying the groceries we needed, we took a cab back to the gate and transferred our groceries into another cab on the other side of the gate then we got in that cab and were driven to our home. It was all a little crazy but it was what it was.

It is important to future stories in this book to describe our house. The house was made of concrete blocks and had a flat concrete roof. The concrete block sides on the outside and in the interior of the house had been smooth with more concrete then painted. All dividing and connecting walls inside the house were also made of concrete blocks. We had a regular toilet in the bathroom but the shower/tub was square made of concrete blocks which had then been smoothed and tiled.

All windows opened by sliding them side to side and there was one thumb screw in the center to lock them when closed. Screens on all of the windows were made of blue plastic fabric. Wooden "stealy" bars covered all of the windows on the outside of the house but were easy to pull off one wooden bar at a time.

Both of the doors to the house swung open to the outside which also left the hinge pins exposed on the outside of the house. Our screen doors were on the inside of the doorway and opened to the inside. I do not a clue as to the reason for things being backward but at the time I just excepted it.

We had a fence all around the house which was about five feet high and made of the same concrete blocks. On the road side of our home, we had a rolling chain-linked, twelve-foot gate that when open rolled in a track against the concrete fence. Actually, the gate was wider than the concrete driveway which allowed us to pull a car into that driveway easily when the gate was open. I think this all pretty much describes our home, yard, and fence with the gate.

The house was not air-conditioned but we bought one box fan and an oscillating fan on a stand. In the winter time, we had one free-standing kerosene heater. We did not have a telephone but we did have a Sony portable TV that had an eight-inch screen on it with a pull out antenna. It also had a snap on cover that protected the TV screen. I had brought the TV with me as a carry-on on my plane trip from the States.

Frank and I settled into playing house again and you would think that we had never been apart. We loved Okinawa — it was a beautiful island. The Okinawan people were always smiling and were really happy people. They had very little but they made do with what they had which made Frank and I fit in perfectly. After all, we only needed each other.

32

uneven numbers competition

Frank only had a week off from his job at Torii Station to help me get settled into our new home. We worked really hard to get settled in and we did it.

Frank worked thirty days straight of each shift, days, evenings then nights, with a couple of days off between the different shifts.

The day shift was worked from the hours from 6:00 A.M. until 3:00 P.M., the evening shift was worked from 3:00 P.M. until 11:00 P.M. and the night shift was worked from 11:00 P.M. until 6:00 A.M.

Since Frank and I did not have yet have children, I adjusted my schedule to his schedule. If Frank worked all night I stayed up all night working on things around the house then I slept with him during the day.

Sometimes after I met some of the wives around me who were also without children, we would have "Wife All Night Parties" at different homes. We would strip floors, make curtains, make fudge, and cook up meals to put in the freezers of our refrigerators.

Of course, the night shift was always the hardest for Frank because he was a true morning person. He loved to get up before the sun came up, have coffee sitting outside, and watch the sunrise.

The next story is about the first afternoon after one of those thirty-day long night shifts.

Frank finally had a couple of days off. After getting home at 6:30 A.M., he asked me to make sure I got him up before 3:00 P.M., so we could do something fun together that afternoon. When I woke Frank up he was just a tad bit grouchy, so I made him something to eat. I asked what he would like to drink but he just told me that he would get it himself. Knowing that he was still tired, I just smiled at him and let him do what he wanted to do.

Frank got a drinking glass out of the cabinet above the counter, opened the refrigerator, came out with a bottle of beer in his hand, opened a drawer in the counter, and got the "church key" bottle/can opener. I just kind of stood in the doorway watching him wishing he had slept just a little longer.

If you do not know what a church key bottle/can opener is, it is a stainless steel flat object about five inches long and slightly bent on each end. One end is very pointed for opening lids of cans and the rounded end is for taking lids off of bottles. Frank tried to open the beer bottle but the can/bottle opener kept slipping.

After about five times at trying to get the cap off of the beer bottle, Frank had lost all patience with the opener then he threw it at the sink across the room as hard as he could. (Remember I told you he was a tad bit grouchy.) Karma was not on Frank's side that day, as a matter of fact, karma was still asleep in our bed where Frank should have been sleeping too.

The church key opener missed the sink but hit the wall made of concrete behind the sink, bounced off the wall then came shooting back at Frank then that pointed end of the opener stuck him in the center of the forehead right above his eyebrows quickly falling to the floor. A trickle of blood then came running down from Frank's forehead, running down the middle of his nose then dripple-dropped to the floor.

While silently standing there watching this whole scenario, I was fighting back laughter but the humor and awe of it all along with that drop of blood dripping to the floor overtook me then I started laughing loudly. Frank turned and looked at me with that of blood going down his nose with a tiny drip at the end then asked, "Do you think that was funny Nancy Lou?"

Laughing too hard to answer, I just shook my head up and down for "Yes" then Frank smiled at me as he picked up the drinking glass that he had set on the countertop into his hand then extended his arm and held the drinking glass out to his side away from me.

Still smiling with his big ole dimples, Frank quietly asked me, "Do you think this is funny Nancy Lou?" then he dropped the drinking glass to the tiled floor and it broke into pieces.

Oh my goodness! Well now, Frank knew that I hated uneven numbers of things. We had eight drinking glasses, eight of each kind of silverware, eight plates, eight cups and on and on and on. Odd numbers of things just did not seem right to me but a little like a lonely spare tire.

With my best smile, I walked to the countertop reached into the cabinet above it, pulled out another drinking glass, held it in my hand, stepped back from the counter, extended my arm straight out, and dropped the drinking glass to the tile floor where it immediately shattered into pieces.

Looking at my smiling husband I said, "Frank now we have an "Even Number" of six drinking glasses!"

Trying not to laugh, Frank opened the cabinet took out another glass then proceeded to repeat his first drinking glass drop-on-the-floor-shatter-breaking-thangy with another drinking glass and said, "Nancy Lou now we have an odd number of five drinking glasses."

I took another glass out of the cabinet, extended my arm then dropped it onto the floor. I smiled at my husband who was watching me and laughing loudly as I told him, "Guess what, Frank? Now we have an even number of four drinking glasses!"

Frank and I broke all eight of our drinking glasses that day! Not sure why we did but we were laughing so hard at the end of the total demolition of the drinking glasses that we forgot we had to clean that broken glass mess up.

Nobody really won the competition because all of our drinking glasses were broken. Of course, we were both barefoot so we had to climb up on the counter then crawl along the top to get to the laundry room where the broom and dustpan were located. We cleaned up the mess together, I doctored Frank's wound on his head, then we ate some supper.

Of course, we had to drink our beverages out of our coffee cups for months until we could afford to buy new drinking glasses.

When we did buy new drinking glasses we actually decided we should get an even number, ten drinking glasses. I really wanted sixteen so we could hide a set away in case of needing to have another competition but Frank said we couldn't do that again.

We spent the evening making up from a fight we didn't really have because making up was so much fun and we looked for any reason to do the makeup thangy.

We were nineteen years old, we had been married nearly a year, and we were definitely growing in maturity. Can you tell?

Looking back though, I really think there may have been a winner of the competition. Isn't zero and even number?

The next day Frank and I made a sack lunch and walked to the China Seawall which was about a mile from our home. We walked along the man-made beach and since the tide was out there were many pools of water in the coral reefs with beautiful small brightly colored fish.

Frank and I loved to walk along the China Sea beach and we also climbed up to the tops cliffs made from the coral. These cliffs were covered in huge vines of ivy and other tropical plant growth.

Okinawa is a truly beautiful Island with the white beaches of the Pacific Ocean on one side and the beautiful coral beaches of the China Sea on the opposite side. At one point on the Island, these two bodies of water are only separated by two miles of land and you can see both of them at the same time.

I will never forget the beauty of Okinawa.

33

ralph and ole bondo

Frank and I had settled into the daily living in Okinawa. Okinawa was such a beautiful island. We had made new friends with couples living in homes around us on three different sides which were designated as off-base military housing. Across the road, in front of our home, was an area which was not a part of off-base military housing but had homes of Okinawan families. Both of us felt that we were so lucky to be living in a home that touched different cultures depending on which way you faced or looked. Frank and I loved this so much.

The single soldiers who lived on the base at Torii and worked with Frank came to see us fairly regularly for some home-cooked meals which delighted both of us. They were far away from home and their families, so we had become their new family.

After making friends with two little Okinawan boys and their mom who lived across the road from Frank and me, if I made cookies for Frank, those two little boys would always seem to know. I think the whole neighborhood could smell those cookies cooking.

When the cookies were done, I always walked outside with a plate full of them. When getting to the edge of the house, I would see those two little boys sitting on top of the fence waiting for me to come outside. Their mom was always at the door of their home watching for me too. She would shake her head up and down to let me know it was okay for them to have the cookies. I really loved this.

Frank and I took lots of walks to the China Sea beach in the afternoons when he was working days. On one occasion as we were walking near the coral cliffs we heard some tiny yelps which sounded pretty desperate. As Frank pulled some of the vegetation away from the bottom of the cliff, there was a small cave about as big around as a small car tire. The sound we heard was coming from inside the cave.

Frank decided to crawl into the cave to investigate. Once inside the cave, he found three small puppies hidden away, crying, and obviously abandoned by their momma for some reason. Frank decided to pull them all out of the cave. All of the puppies looked very thin, weak, and wanted their momma.

As we stood there holding the puppies, Frank and I saw the body of their momma lying motionless in the vegetation nearby. She had passed away trying to get to her babies. I was longing to take them home with us which Frank could see all over my face. He smiled at me then said, "Nancy, we need to take these puppies home with us. They need a new momma to take care of them. What do you think?" I didn't answer but jumped for joy while holding one of the puppies in my arms then I gave Frank the biggest hug and kiss!

We carried the puppies back to our home then we hand fed them milk by dipping a torn piece of a sheet gathered into a cone shape dipping the tip into the milk for them to nurse on. Frank and I fed these puppies this way night and day for two weeks until they could eat soft food. When they were strong, two of our neighbors decided they wanted one of the puppies, so we let them each have one but the third puppy, a male, we kept as our own.

We named our puppy, Ralph and he was awesome. Ralph was a beautiful puppy with white hair with a tail that curled up onto his back. We found canned dog food at a little Okinawan store a couple of blocks from our house which he liked but his favorite thing to eat was leftovers from the fridge.

Frank and I always took him with us when we walked to the China Sea beach. He loved to run up and down the beach with us. Ralph could run faster than any dog I could remember ever having. After we bought a car we actually clocked

Ralph running thirty miles an hour in front of that car. He was like a lightning bolt darting and dancing down the beach.

The single GIs loved Ralph as much as we did and would bring him things to play with that he shook and tore to shreds. The little Okinawan boys would climb our fence every day to play with Ralph. I think they loved Ralph even more than my homemade cookies.

The only problem we had with Ralph was that he loved leather. He not only liked to chew on leather but he actually ate leather. Any shoes we had that were made of leather had to be put high up in the closet or he would totally shred them then eat them in what seemed like seconds. In another story to come, you will read about another incident involving leather shoes.

Ralph loved Frank and me as much as we loved him. He was an excellent guard dog and would attack snakes if they got into the yard. Not a person, reptile, or any other animal came into our yard unless he thought they should be there. Many times we had to save papa-sans and mama-sans carrying baskets on their heads full of their homemade wares. They were only trying to open the gate to come inside the yard to get to our door to sell their homemade goodies.

Ralph will come up in many more stories but I want you to know how we found him and how much we loved him.

When some friends of ours were leaving Okinawa to go home to the states, they had a car that they had to get rid of, so Frank and I decided to buy it from them. They sold it to us for \$30.^{00}. It was old but it ran and we thought it was amazing. The following story is about that car.

Some things are not pretty to look at but you just learn to love them and they become priceless. "Ole Bondo" was one of those ugly inanimate creatures. It was a car that had more grey Bondo filler on it than paint. Since it was originally painted light grey before the outside holes had been filled with Bondo, it really wasn't that noticeable.

The tires were slick with very little tread on them, so we tried to not drive to fast in the rain. Of course, there were other reasons to drive slowly in the rain too. The front seat was held up by a two by four which had been placed under it because the floorboards had some very iffy with large holes in them.

Heavy cardboard had been laid on either side of the front floorboards which prevented junk from flying into the car as it was driven. Of course, the cardboard also prevented the rainwater from flying into the car from the road if it was raining. Sometimes the cardboard would have to be taken out to let it dry for a while if we drove it in heavy rain.

If the wind blew hard or if it rained hard when the car was parked the lights would come on mysteriously by themselves, so we always unplugged the battery at night. There was also some weird electrical problem going on with the headlights, brake lights, taillights and blinkers when we drove the car. Frank and I learned to roll down the windows to use hand signals while driving to do turns and brakes signals.

We tried not to drive it too much at night because the headlights would suddenly go off by themselves for a brief moment but they always suddenly came back on. Even with all of its quirky ailments, Frank and I loved "Ole Bondo".

Finally after several months, Frank and a friend of his totally rewired the whole car. It was simply amazing how many wires were broken and had to be replaced. They worked on it in the evenings when they were working day shifts and after a few weeks, Ole Bondo did not do its quirky electrical fun things.

We could actually use the blinkers, the headlights, the brake lights, and the taillights actually worked right. This was truly amazing!

The next thing they did was to get another friend to weld some pieces of metal to the front floorboards because the cardboard was getting a little mushy and stinky. Also, this totally prevented our feet from getting wet if driving while it rained. Now we could go barefoot in the car without worrying about junk flying up from the road to hit our feet.

The two by four remained under the front seat but good grief you can't have all the luxuries in life. Although, we thought about spray-painting the car one color but decided that we would have to then change its name. Why would we do that?

I am not sure what kind of car this was but as far as I am concerned it was an "Ole Bondo."

34

ralph's love of leather

I have told you about finding our sweet dog, Ralph, and how much he loved leather but I have not shared with you the things he could do to things made of it.

Frank and I were given a Bible by his grandmother, whom we called Gram on Christmas Eve in 1968. The Bible was made of white leather with our names engraved in gold on the bottom of the front cover. We dearly loved this Bible. I had carried it with me in my suitcase to Okinawa.

We had a small coffee table in our living room and our Bible laid on this table on top of a doily which was an ornamental mat we had purchased made of crochet yarn.

After Ralph got past the small puppy stage, he would jump up on the couch next to the coffee table to sleep. One day while I was in the kitchen washing dishes, Ralph decided to do more than sleep. When I returned to the living room Ralph had eaten half of the cover off of our Bible but not just the front of the cover but the back was nearly all eaten away.

Frank and my names were totally gone from the front of the Bible. I looked around the couch for pieces of the Bible cover but there were not any pieces anywhere. We had forgotten the Bible had a leather cover on it but Ralph had sniffed it then eaten most of the cover. I was devastated but I knew it was our faults for not putting it in the closet high up on a shelf with all of our leather shoes.

Frank and I kept the Bible and I still have it. Of course, it is a continuing reminder of our sweet Ralph and how much we loved him.

The next story is about another adventure of Ralph's and his leather loving antics. I laugh every time this story comes to my mind.

Frank and I had invited some of his single GI friends to come over to our home to spend the day. I had made cookies and fudge for them to snack on and I had plans to make homemade spaghetti and meat sauce. Frank and his buddies had just finished working thirty days of the day shift.

They were all ready to have some fun which meant getting off of the Torii Base. We would play cards, listen to music, and eat. The single guys would bring beer, snacks, cokes (coca cola) and liquor for those if they wanted they wanted mixed drinks. They always helped us cook, clean up, and wash the dishes.

Since I had stripped the floors with lye water then waxed them with clear wax which made the floors shine as if they were brand new, the guys always took their shoes off at the door as a respectful gesture for my hard work and to not mess up the floors.

Frank told me that a new soldier was coming who had just arrived in Okinawa from the states and who was feeling really homesick. I was so glad he was going to come with the other guys. We were all far away from home but we had become a true family.

When they all arrived, the guys spent some time outside playing with Ralph then they came inside. Frank and I made sure Ralph stayed outside so that they could take off their shoes without him eating them if the shoes were made of leather.

Once they all came inside, one of the GIs showed Frank and I a pair of shoes he had worn that he had made special by the Okinawans to fit his feet perfectly. They were made of leather, with beautiful detail on them and were really beautiful shoes. Of course, he took them off and left them inside by the front door with all of the other GI's shoes.

We all went into the bedroom which Frank and I had made into a stereo room after we had bought a reel-to-reel, amp, and speakers for our birthdays. We dearly loved that room and spent a lot of time in there listening to music since we did not have a television. Also, we could go to the base where we could record reels of music for free, we had a lot of reels of music.

Frank and I had taken the doors off of the closet then I had made a large padded cushion for the floor of the closet, covered it with some fabric then we painted the cover for the outlet socket low in the closet which was really for a moisture rod which heated up to keep mold out of the closet but since there weren't any clothes in the closet we replaced the rod with a light bulb. The effects of the light coming through the round holes in the cover was amazing.

The new GI really got into relaxing with us all and enjoying himself which made us all very happy. He decided to go outside to get something out of the car they had all ridden into our house. When he returned, he had a present for Frank and I which was a beautiful knick-knack that he had bought in Okinawa.

After a while, I decided to go into the kitchen to cook some lunch but was in for a big surprise as I entered the living room from the stereo room. Ralph was sitting in the living room by the front door next to the shoes. Immediately, I called for Frank to come to the kitchen. When Frank came through the door, being speechless at what at what my eyes were seeing, all that I could do was point towards Ralph.

Frank started laughing loudly, then he said, "Who let Ralph in the house?"

I whispered to Frank that it was not funny and to quit laughing but he paid me no mind at all then the GI who had gone out to the car to get the present for us answered, "I did. Ralph really looked like he wanted to come inside."

Well, that answer made Frank laugh even louder with tears in his eyes which brought all of the guys into the living room. Frank pointed towards Ralph and they all started laughing at what they saw by the front door. Ralph had totally devoured one of the GI's special made leather shoes and was working on eating the other one.

Thinking Frank and the guys had drunk far too much beer, I asked them if they knew that Ralph had eaten some specially made shoes but that just made them laugh more. Even the GI who owned the shoes was laughing loudly, so I just decided to laugh with them. Evidently, these guys loved Ralph so much that he could do no wrong in their eyes.

Frank and I offered to pay for the shoes but the GI told us that he would not let us because he had so much fun at our house and he had two pairs made.

Ralph loved to eat leather and the bible which remains in my possession today reminds me of our first amazing child dog.

Praying you are chasing butterflies, running faster than a speeding bullet, have an endless supply of leather and playing with your amazing dad, Frank. I love you for eternity, Ralph.

35

leather

In late September of 1969, Typhoon Elsie was in the Pacific Ocean heading towards Okinawa. Living in approved Military Off-Base housing, Frank was released to be at home with me until all threat of it hitting Okinawa had ended. Frank and I were originally from the Gulf Coast of Texas, so we were educated as to what to do and how to prepare for a Hurricane. We decided a Typhoon would not be much different, so we prepared accordingly.

What could possibly happen?

Our home was made of concrete blocks which made it very sturdy. Inside the wooden-stealy bars that were on all windows, there were wooden shutters that slid shut which meant we would not have to figure out a way to protect the windows. The doors on the house were metal without windows, so flying debris would have a hard time trying to penetrate them.

Frank and I had purchased nonperishable groceries: canned spam, canned chili, crackers, cheese, canned pork and beans, sardines, and canned milk. We also bought a small folding sterno stove, small cans of sterno, batteries for our radio, candles, and matches. I cleaned the kitchen sink to hold water and filled every large container we had with water for drinking.

Frank had parked Ole Bondo next to the house which faced North because the driveway faced South towards the China Sea. We had decided the house would block the worst winds from hitting the car. After the house and car were secure, we pulled the mattress off our bed and put it in the living room. Frank, Ralph, and I would weather the storm in the center of our home with all doors to other rooms closed.

After our home was secure, we decided to walk to the China Seawall and the man-made beach one more time to see how high the waves were before we hunkered down inside our home. The sea was really rough and the power of the typhoon churning the water was threatening but beautiful. We took some pictures then we walked back to our home and settled in for the evening and night.

Frank and I had made a Typhoon tracking map from four large pieces of paper which we had taped together. We played cards while listening to the radio for the latest coordinates of the storm to plot them on our map. Being too excited to sleep, when the lights suddenly went off in the middle of the night, we lit candles for some light. We decided it would be best to sleep in shifts so that one of us would be awake to plot the newest coordinates.

As soon as it was morning, we could hear the wind picking up and roaring outside the house. Frank suddenly remembered an important thing we had forgotten to do. "Ole" Bondo was protected from harm but not the wind and we had forgotten to unplug the battery to keep the headlights from coming on which would drain the battery so the car would not start. This would happen every time it rained or the wind blew, so we always kept the battery unplugged when we weren't driving the car.

Of course, the wind suddenly gusted and howled loudly as Frank said, "Nancy Lou, I am going outside to unplug the battery in the car."

I looked at him in disbelief then told him, "Frank, you are not going outside in the wind and rain while a Typhoon is headed this way."

Frank laughed loudly as he ran then opened the front door of the house, held on to the door then pushed it hard to close it as he disappeared from my site. I could actually hear him laughing loudly over the loud howling of the wind as he ran around the corner of the house to get to Ole Bondo.

Finally in what seemed like hours but was only a few minutes, I heard him at the front door. Frank opened the door but a gust of wind grabbed the door which swung open to the outside of the house. He was holding on to the door trying to pull it closed behind him when the next gust of wind ripped the door off of its hinges, nearly hitting Frank as he let go of it. The door went flying down our driveway as Frank ran into the house.

I looked at Frank, who had suddenly stopped his laughing, then said, "Really, Frank? What are we gonna do for a front door now? You know what that screen door will not keep the wind and rain out."

Frank said, "Nancy Lou, have no fear, I am going to get my hammer, some nails then go outside to nail the door back into the door frame."

Pretty sure the look I gave him was not a pleasing one as I shook my head side to side but before I could speak, Frank ran to the laundry room, grabbed the hammer and some nails, then went out the back door.

With the wind gusting, Frank drug the door back to the house then stood it up trying to fight against the wind as he tried to put it back into the door frame. The wind kept pushing him backward, so I decided to run out the back door and help him. It took both of us to get that door back in the frame. I held it while Frank nailed the door shut.

We were both totally soaked from the rain as we crawled our way to the back door to get back inside the house but once inside the house, we both could not stop laughing. We were a fearless team and probably being only nineteen kinda helped.

Frank and I survived the Typhoon Elsie. Frank had to go back to work at the base two days later when the threat to the Island ended. Since he would be working night shifts and the front door had not been fixed yet, we just used the back door.

Since Frank was working the night shift, I invited a girlfriend of mine over to stay the night. We cooked some supper then made some of my famous fudge. After we had eaten we were listening to music on the stereo when Ralph started to bark loudly out in the backyard.

Earlier I had let Ralph outside the back door so he could to run around and do his business. The front porch light was on because in Okinawa we had what were called "Stealy Boys". A quick explanation of "Stealy Boys": they dressed all in black, had razor blades sown into their clothes, moved like ninjas, and could get into your home quickly and quietly. We were warned to never engage them, never try to stop them and to act like we were asleep if they entered our homes.

Since Ralph was in the backyard on the side of our home without windows, I could not see him or what he was barking at. I asked my girlfriend if she thought it could be "Stealy Boys" when she didn't answer me, I looked at her and could see the fear in her face.

Frank and I did not have a porch light next to the back door and I knew that the back door was the only way to get out or into the house. The fear on my friends face made me feel protective of her, angry at our situation, and brought out my fearlessness. We did not have a phone or a car, if we had to escape the front door was nailed shut, and the only way out was through the back door. I decided to just go to the back door, open it then look into the backyard.

As I started to open the back door, I heard Ralph barking on the driveway near the front door. Instead of opening the back door, I ran to the window by the front door. Looking out the window, I saw Ralph barking at a snake on our driveway. It was such a relief to see the snake, even though I DO NOT like snakes.

Laughing, I told my girlfriend, "It is just a snake."

She asked me, "Is it a *habu*?"

I asked her, "What is a *habu*?"

She explained to me that *habus* were very venomous snakes that lived on the island. Suddenly, I realized that my precious Ralph was attacking a venomous snake, so I ran to the window, opened it, and tried to get Ralph to get away from the snake but he wouldn't.

The snake was crawling towards the front door, so I asked my girlfriend to watch it from the window while I ran to the bedroom. After quickly putting on Frank's black combat boots, I ran back to the living room then asked my girlfriend where the snake was. She told me that it was in front of the front door.

I positioned myself in front of the inside of the door then with all of my strength I kicked the door with one of my booted feet. To my surprise, the door fell loudly to the ground landing on the driveway. Now, I had to lift up the door to see if the snake had been killed. Before that happened, Ralph ran past the door to the fence barking at the snake that was going under the gate out into the road.

My girlfriend and I started jumping up and down cheering on the driveway. We were about to walk to the door when we heard a car drive into the next door neighbors driveway. Suddenly out of nowhere three people dressed all in black jumped the fence into my yard, ran across the front yard faster than a speeding bullet then jumped the fence on the other side of the house.

My girlfriend and I stood there frozen and speechless staring across the yard at the fence until we heard the neighbors come to the fence behind us and ask us what we were doing. We told them all about the snake and the obvious "Stealy Boys" who had just jumped the fence between their house and mine.

The neighbors checked their home but nothing was missing then they helped us put the front door back up and nail it into the door frame. After we thanked the neighbors, Ralph, my girlfriend, and I went back inside the house through the back door then we listened to music waiting for our husbands to get home.

When Frank got home, I excitedly told him all about what had happened during the night. After I was finished talking he said, "Nancy, I love you with all of my heart but sometimes your fearlessness really scares me. You didn't mess up my boots, did you? Do I need to punish you by making you spit shine them?"

Of course then Frank ran and I had to put on those black combat boots then chase him around the yard!

Frank fixed the front door that morning before he slept even though I asked him not to but I knew in my heart why he did.

Typhoon Elsie, habu, and "Stealy Boys," it just didn't get better than that on Okinawa in late September of 1969.

36

pizza party

It was now October of 1969 and we did not have any more typhoons, habus or flying doors. The "Stealy Boys" would always be a threat but Frank and I had learned to live with that.

On October 4, 1969, Frank turned twenty-years-old then on October 6, 1969, I also turned twenty-years-old. The single GIs that were our close friends invited us to go out to dinner with them. They took us to a fancy restaurant in Naha, Okinawa.

When we got to the restaurant and once inside, we were seated on three sides of a large U-shaped bar that had bar stools around it. There was a large grill in the middle of the U-shape which actually attached to the three sides of the bar. An opening behind the grill was for the *itamae* (chef).

As we sat there watching the *itamae* cook for us, I was totally amazed at the way he used his knives to cut, toss, turn then flip the food onto our individual plates. We were all served Kobe beef which is absolutely the most tender, moist, melt-in-your-mouth meat I have ever eaten.

The itamae put real butter on the grill with garlic then added a huge chunk of Kobe beef the size of a large roast on top of the butter then the fun started as he used his knives to cut, toss and turn the meat while also doing vegetables on the other side of the grill.

He asked how we wanted our meat cooked and when he had it cooked just the way we wanted it, he flipped small chunks of it onto our plates in seconds. Vegetables grilled in butter and garlic were then flipped on to our plates too. The Itamae saved the bean sprouts for last which were also done in butter and garlic. I can not think of a good enough word to describe the taste of bean sprouts, except totally awesome.

We also had sake which was served warm in small oriental ceramic cups. Sake is made from fermented rice starch water converted to sugar then added yeast which once fermented makes it into an alcoholic drink. Just believe me when I tell you, you do not need to drink but a little of this at one time.

Frank and I were so grateful to the single GIs for buying us such an amazing meal for our birthdays. We thanked them over and over knowing neither of us would ever forget that meal or could ever have afforded it. They told us we were more than welcome and they couldn't wait to eat some more home cooked meals at our home. Pretty sure my cooking did not come close to matching that of the itamae.

Talking about food, let's go on to the next story.

Frank was getting ready to go to work on his last evening shift meaning he would have a day off the next day when he asked me how I was feeling. I told him great and if he wanted to he could invite the single GIs over after work for some homemade late night pizza. I was so excited for Frank to finally have a day off and the single guys were always fun to have around. They reminded me so much of my four brothers who were so far away. Since it would be late after they ate, they would all end up crashing on the living room floor then Frank and I would cook them breakfast the next morning.

After Frank left for work in Ole Bondo, I cleaned up the house then started making yeast dough for the crust of the pizzas. While the dough was going through its rising process, I cooked some hamburger in the skillet then drained the grease off and put it into a bowl. We didn't have pepperoni, sausage or ham but we did have cans of that "mystery meat" called spam, so I opened three cans of spam and cut that mystery meat up into chunks then put it into another bowl.

I made pizza sauce then while it was simmering in the pan on the stove, chopped up some onions then used my hand-grater to grate a large chunk of cheese. We did not have pizza pans but I had four large cookie sheets. Since the pizza dough was ready to spread out into the pans, I split the dough into four pieces then spread it out covering the bottoms and edges of each pan.

Next, I spooned the pizza sauce onto the top of the dough in each pan, spreading it out to the edges, added to each pan equally the hamburger, chunked spam, onions, and topped it off the grated cheese then put the pizzas into to the refrigerator until time to cook them.

After washing then drying the dishes and cleaning up the mess that was made, I went into the living room and sat down for a while then after a few minutes, got up to go see if the clothes were dry on the clothesline. Since it had been raining for days, Frank and I had put up some clotheslines in one of the spare bedrooms next to the washroom. The clothes were dry, so I folded them then put them away where they belonged.

A couple of days earlier, I had come down with a cold with a slight fever which was making me kind of tired so I went back to the living and sat back down. Frank was such a worry wart about me that I could not let him know if I was not feeling well because then he would make me go to bed. So, I had really tried to hide my cold from him.

Frank would be getting off from work at 11:00 p.m. which meant he would be home around 11:30 p.m. with our friends. Since we had a very small apartment size oven, at 11:00 p.m. I started cooking the pizzas two at a time. I kept thinking and worrying about Frank driving in the rain because of those slick tires on Ole Bondo. It seemed like the rain was getting heavier every time I looked out of our front door.

After the pizzas were done, I looked at the clock and knew that Frank and the guys would be arriving any minute. Thirty more minutes passed by but Frank was not home then I began to really worry. We did not have a telephone and Frank had driven our only car to work.

At 12:30 a.m., I could not wait any longer. We had some friends that lived down near the China Seawall, so I decided to walk to their home. I didn't have a flashlight or an umbrella, so I just went like I was. The husband of these friends worked with Frank and was on the same shift, so I prayed that he and his wife were still awake.

After practically running the whole way to our friends home, after I finally got to their door, the lights were still on in their home. I knocked on the door and the husband answered. He looked a little shocked to see me standing there soaking wet but asked me to come inside then ran to get a towel so I could dry off a little.

Anxious but trying to stay calm, I told him why I had come to his home. Without hesitation, he told me that he would drive me to Torii Base and we would search along the route for any cars that might have slid off the road.

All the way to Torii Station, we searched but did not see any cars off of the road. When we arrived at the base, he drove to the building where he and Frank worked, parked the car then went inside. While he was inside the building, I sat in the car and searched the parking lot with my eyes for our car but it was not there.

Finally, after a few minutes, our friend came out of the building then told me that Frank was not in the building but he was okay and he would drive me back home.

I looked at him in disbelief while saying, "Where is he? Where is our car? I am really scared. Please, take me to him."

He looked at me with concern in his eyes then said, "Nancy, it's okay, I will take you to him."

We only went three blocks in his car when we arrived at the Service Men's Club. Sitting in the parking lot parked near the front door of the club sat Ole Bondo. I looked at our friend and I am sure that he saw the combined look of relief yet the fire of fury in my eyes.

He told me, "Nancy, you stay put. I will go inside and send Frank out to you. You are all wet still. Anyway, I think I need a beer."

Have you ever been so relieved but so upset with someone that you just have trouble breathing? That was me at that very moment but I decided to get out of our friend's car, walk over to then get into Ole Bondo. I got into the driver's seat and waited.

Frank emerged from the building smiling with those killer dimples, weaving down the sidewalk. Once he got to the car, Frank opened the passenger door and climbed into the seat, closing the door once he was in. I stretched my arm towards him with hand palm up then he gave me the keys to the car which I started then backed the car up. The car was so quiet you could hear a pin drop as we started the drive home when out of nowhere Frank broke the silence.

Frank: "Nancy, are you mad at me?"

Me: (silence; thinking, "Just a tad")

Frank: "Why are you all wet?"

Me: (silence; thinking, "Maybe walking a mile in the rain?")

Frank: "How's your cold?"

Me: (silence; thinking, "Could be better, Mister.")

Frank: "Come on Nancy, why don't you just yell at me are something?"

Me: (silence; thinking, "Not going to, trying to avoid those dimples. Anyway, this is more fun.")

Frank: "I'm sorry, we were just going to have one beer then we lost track of the time."

Me: (silence; thinking, "Maybe you need a new watch?")

Frank: "Please, look at me."

Me: (silence; thinking, "Not gonna look at those melt me Dimples.")

Frank: "Nancy, please talk to me."

Me: (silence; thinking, "Why this is working out so well")

Frank: "I love you, Nancy"

Me: (silence; thinking, "Dang it Frank, you nearly broke my silence. Thank God we are home.")

Finally, I drove the car into the driveway at our home. We got out of the car and walked into the house with me trying my best not to look at Frank or laugh. I wanted so much to tell him how much I loved him but knowing if I looked at him he would melt me with those dimples.

While walking through the kitchen then stopping at our bedroom door, I pointed at the pizzas on the kitchen counter then broke my silence by saying, "There's your supper, Frank."

After entering the bedroom then closing the bedroom door, I put my head into the pillow on our bed to muffle my laughter. I loved this dimple-faced man, was so thankful that he was okay, and really just wanted to run back to that kitchen then hug him tightly.

Suddenly, Frank yelled from the kitchen, "Great pizza, Nancy! Do I have to sleep on the couch? The couch is kinda small!"

I turned off the bedroom light and walked to the bedroom door opening it so Frank would know where he could sleep then I got into our bed waiting for him to come to bed. Frank stumbled to the bed, laid down, and I scooted over next to him taking my position by him laying my head on his chest with his arm wrapped around me then said, "I love you so much, Frank Henderson" but he didn't hear me because he was already peacefully asleep and soon I was peacefully asleep by his side.

Frank and I were lost in sleep until I was suddenly awakened by loud singing outside our bedroom window. I shook Frank to wake him. Frank was groggy but he quickly sat up in bed.

When we looked out the window, there they were, our single GI friends, sitting in a circle in our yard singing and drinking Akadama wine, a cheap red wine, in the rain. Frank and I started laughing as we ran to the front door to get outside to quieten them down so they wouldn't wake the whole world.

After we got them inside the house, one of them told me through his slurring that they had come to tell me that it was their fault that Frank had not come home on time because they kept buying him beers and that they were all really sorry.

I started laughing then told them all, "Frank is a big boy and you are not to blame. Anyway, he is not in trouble. I am just so thankful he is okay. Now let's talk about you all singing loudly in the front yard at 5:00 in the morning but first let me fix you all some breakfast. How about cold pizza?"

After Frank and I made them a real breakfast of eggs, bacon, and biscuits with homemade gravy, they all passed out in sleep all over the living room. We covered them up with blankets then Frank and I went back to bed.

As we laid there, Frank smiled at me with those amazing dimples and it was all good.

37

mayo jars, christmas, moving

Octber of 1969 was passing by quickly for Frank and me in Okinawa. We had met lots of couples who lived around us in off-base housing and had become friends with an Okinawan family that lived across the street from our home.

Sometimes while Frank was at work, I would see the *mama-san* cleaning her home after her children and the *papa-san* had left for work. She would drag all of their furniture out into the yard then sweep and actually washout the whole house. All of the mats that they slept on were shaken and then hung out on the fence to air.

The mama-san did not speak very much English and all I knew in Okinawan was *moshi moshi* which meant "hello" on the telephone, only when I said it sounded more like "mushey mushey" but somehow we learned to communicate by using our hand gestures and smiles.

One day, she invited me to come into her home then showed me all of the rooms inside. It was truly an awesome sight. The family did not have beds to sleep on or chairs to sit in. Beautiful mats were on the floors in all of the rooms in the house and a short-legged table which was big enough to seat the entire family around it, set in the largest room.

Mama-san was very sweet but papa-san had a little problem which was his love of sake.

Frank was working days, which meant he had to get up very early in the mornings to get to work at Torii Station. We had gone to bed around 10:00 p.m. but in the wee hours of the morning we were awakened by pounding and yelling sounds which were coming from outside the house.

Frank and I got up to look out of our bedroom window and saw papa-san beating on the metal door to his home across the street from our home. Papa-san was yelling loudly at the door. It was very evident that mama-san had locked her husband out of their home and for a very good reason. Papa-san had a sake bottle in his hand and was very drunk.

Amused, we watched from our bedroom window for a while but after he sat down in front of the door, we went back to bed. Just as we were in the midst of falling back asleep, new noises started from outside. Our front gate was being shaken, there was loud singing, and Ralph began barking loudly all of which woke us up again,

We jumped out of the bed and looked out of the bedroom window again. Papa-san was awake, shaking our gate, and singing loudly. Finally, after a few minutes, papa-san stopped shaking our gate, walked back to his home then sat down in front of the door again.

After calming Ralph down, we were headed back to bed when suddenly we heard a bottle crash against our fence. Evidently, papa-san had finished drinking his bottle of sake and had decided to throw the empty bottle at our fence. Not amused, Frank got out of the bed then walked out of the bedroom heading into our kitchen telling me, "Nancy, I have had enough of this!"

I followed Frank to the kitchen to see what he was up to. He opened one of the kitchen cabinets then took out an empty mayonnaise jar that I had washed and saved. I asked him, "Frank what are you doing?"

Definitely, on a mission of his own, Frank did not answer me but just laughed as he walked to our back door carrying the mayo jar in his hand, opened the door, and went outside. I followed closely behind him because I knew he was fixing to do something that would either go horribly wrong or be totally amazing but either way very memorable.

After he was outside, Frank sat the mayo jar on the roof then he climbed himself up onto the flat roof of our home. I could hear him quietly walking across the roof to the front of our home then there was a loud crashing sound, lots of loud laughter, and Frank came running across the roof of the house and jumping off the roof then he grabbed my arm pulling me into the house with him.

I asked him, "Frank did you hit papa-san with that mayo Jar?"

Frank replied, "Nope! I threw it like a football with a lot of high arc on it. It landed just far enough away to scare him but not close enough to hurt him. He won't be messing with the fence or the gate anymore. He probably thinks that jar fell from the sky above."

We did not hear any more noise from papa-san the rest of the night which was a really good thing. The next morning, I went outside to clean up the glass on the road and discovered mama-san outside beginning to clean the glass up too.

We worked together getting all of the glass picked up and laughing together without any words having to be spoken. After all, we both knew what had happened the night before with our husbands having "The Sake Bottle - Mayo Jar War." Of course, no record of this short war would ever be recorded, so it will not be found in history books, but believe me, it happened.

October ended then November came swiftly and passed by for us in 1969. Frank and I were now facing our first Christmas together without being around our families. Early in December, we bought gifts from the Okinawan stores, boxed them up then mailed them to our families in Texas. We really wanted them to get our gifts before Christmas.

We bought lights at one of the stores in Koza City. They were beautiful lights with Chinese Palace Japanese Oriental covers. I still have the beautiful covers to these lights in my cedar chest. Also, we bought a small tabletop artificial Christmas Tree which already had lights on it and came with small ornaments to put on it.

Frank and I decided that we wanted to invite all of our friends over for Christmas Dinner. Early in December, Frank told everyone at work that we were going to have a big Christmas dinner at our house, to bring their favorite dish, any chairs or folding tables they had, and that we would furnish all of the turkey, dressing, giblet gravy, homemade rolls, sweet potatoes, and fruit salad that they could eat plus boiled custard which is also known in the South as drinking custard which can be served warm or cold, booze or not, and is much like eggnog only better.

I wrote a letter to my grandmother, who I called Ninnie, asking her for all of her recipes. I had always helped but had never cooked an entire Christmas dinner by myself. She wrote me back with all of her recipes for everything I would be making. I have this letter in a box with Frank's letters from Vietnam.

A week before the Christmas dinner, Frank and I went to the commissary on Kadena Air Base where we bought a huge turkey and all of the other groceries that we needed. We really had no idea how many people would show up Christmas Day but we really didn't care, the more the merrier.

A few days before the dinner party, people were bringing chairs, tables, silverware, plates, and tablecloths to our home helping us set up. We moved our living room furniture into our spare bedroom which let us have two huge rooms for all to eat and visit in.

Frank had to work evenings Christmas Eve. He helped me with as much of the preparations for cooking as he could before he left for work but it was quite evident that I would be up all night cooking while listening to the music on the reel-to-reel.

About 9:00 p.m., I took a break and went with Ralph outside for a breather. A papa-san with a bundle on his head came up to the gate motioning to me to come to the gate and let him in the yard then saying, "Mama-son need baskets? I have pretty baskets for you."

Papa-sans and mama-sans had been to our home many times and we had bought some beautiful knick-knacks that they had carved or woven by hand. I decided to look at what he had in his bundle. I motioned to him and he came in the gate, placed the bundle on the ground in front of me then untied it so I could see the treasures that were inside it.

There were so many beautiful things in his bundle, including two oval-shaped baskets of different sizes but one cradled inside the other. Papa-san saw the way I looked at those two baskets then asked, "Mama-san need baskets?"

I told him, "They are beautiful but mama-san has no money today. We are cooking for many people."

He shook his head understanding then bundled up his wares putting the bundle back on his head then went out of the gate closing it behind him then Ralph and I went back into the house.

A couple of hours later, I decided to go back outside with Ralph again and there on the concrete sitting next to the front door were the two baskets that papa-san had left for me. Tears come to my eyes as a type this story remembering the beautiful kindness of a Christmas Eve gift which was totally unexpected being left for me by the amazing soul of papa-san. I would never see him again while on the Island but I will never forget him or his kindness.

The next day, our house was full of people laughing, eating, and having a great time. There was so much food and everyone had brought different dishes of awesome food. The single guys had brought anything they thought we might need and food too.

We ate all day then everyone helped clean up and we all sat in the stereo room I listen to music, laughing, and enjoying a very amazing Christmas Day.

Some of the single GIs ended up crashing in their usual places on the living floor. Thinking they just wanted to be in our home with the warmth of family around them.

Frank and I may not have been with our family in the states but we were with our family in Okinawa. Christmas is about being with family and sometimes it means making friends that become new members of your family.

We were not looking for another home but a couple who we had become best friends with told us about a home that had become available across the street from the entryway to Torii Station. These friends lived in the house next door to the one they told us about. Frank and I were thrilled at having the opportunity to move next door to them, so we rented the new home, packed up our stuff and moved.

Being across the road from Torii Station, meant that Frank could walk the eight blocks to work and I would not have to worry about him driving Ole Bondo in the rain. The only thing that concerned me was making sure that we watched Ralph closely because we would not have a closed-in fence with a gate to keep him safe.

Early spring had come to Okinawa and more fun is to come.

38

stork, water, and a note

Moving across the road from Torii Station then living next to our best friend's home was a whole new beautiful experience. Our home and the neighbors were actually at a hill bottom. Homes behind us were separated from us by a fence then had yards that gradually sloped uphill until they were about twenty feet higher.

Our next door friends had a little boy about six-months-old who we totally fell in love with him. We had lots of married friends and they all had children or the wives of the couples who did not have children were pregnant. It seemed that the Stork was dropping babies every month to others around us but not at our home. We were so happy for them all and would babysit their children doing our best to spoil them. Frank was like a pied piper with children. They knew he loved them and they loved him. Watching Frank talking and playing with children was just beautiful.

Frank and I had never used any type of birth control but I had still not become pregnant. After a year of marriage, each month that passed without me conceiving ended up with me in tears with a feeling like I had failed Frank. Of course, Frank would hold me close telling me that I was wrong and could never fail him but it never changed the way I felt inside. Knowing the beautiful soul and heart of the man I had married. I longed to carry his child, to see his face when his first child was born then watch him being a father.

We decided to make an appointment with one of the obstetricians at Kadena Base for me for a checkup. When Frank and I arrived for the appointment to our surprise there were at least a hundred or more women in all stages of pregnancy sitting or standing in the waiting room. Frank was the only man in the room and I am sure felt a little out of place but he just held my hand and smiled.

Soon my name was called but when I started towards the door to follow the nurse, Frank would not release my hand then said, "Nancy, we are doing this together. I am going in with you."

We walked into the exam room together, Frank sat in a chair while my exam was done then we were led to an office next to the exam room by the doctor. We told him about not being able to conceive. The doctor opened his desk, pulled out a piece of paper called an ovulation chart and a special thermometer then handed them to us while explaining to us how to use the two items. Also, he told us to come back in three months. Frank and I went home then read the back of the ovulation chart and decided we could follow the rules.

Well, all was going well until we got to the days designated as "abstinence." Abstinence is defined as a practice of restraining oneself from indulging in something. Have you ever decided you would not have any candy for a while then it seems like every place you look or go you are confronted with pictures or bowls of candy which overwhelms you so much that you can't and do not want to stop yourself from indulging? I rest my case.

We did our best but when Frank and I returned to the doctor, he was laughing as he told us we had failed the chart abstinence test. Of course, we already knew that. When we got home, we put the chart away and went back to just being Frank and Nancy, living each moment carefree.

The next day was a Saturday and Frank surprised me with two tiny baby kittens. One was a Burmese Siamese that we named Candy. The other kitten that we named Homer was black and white. Candy had such a bend in his tail that it looked like a heart was on the end of it. Homer was special because he had a funny squeak instead of a meow.

Ralph thought they were okay but gave them a little space for a while before he gave up and played with them. Of course, they all ended up on our bed at night even though they had a cozy bed on the floor at the foot of the bed.

Frank and I had so much fun with each other and our playfulness with each other was contagious to our friends. The next story is about one of those moments.

It was a beautiful Summer day in Okinawa, plus it was a Saturday. Since Frank was on his day off, we had slept in later than normal. After we fixed breakfast together, Frank volunteered to wash the dishes while I hung out a load of clothes which I had put into the washer before we fixed breakfast. Frank cranked up the stereo system and music filled the house.

It was really hot and humid outside and it would take a while to hang out the clothes because I was a stickler about how they hung on the clothesline. After putting the clothes in our clothes basket, I walked out our back door which passed by the kitchen window. The kitchen window was open above the sink.

Approaching the window, I could hear the music then saw Frank standing at the sink when he asked, "Lou would you like a cold glass of water when you get through?"

I replied, "Thank you, Frank, that would be great."

While hanging out the clothes, a smile came to my face thinking about how much I loved my dimple-faced husband. In my mind, I knew today was going to be a fun day. It only took about fifteen minutes to hang out the clothes then I picked up the clothes basket and headed back towards the back door.

When I got to the kitchen window, Frank asked, "Lou, are you ready for your glass of cold water?"

I replied, "Yes, I am, it is hot out here."

Suddenly cold water came flying out the window, soaking me from head to toe! Loud laughter came from the window as I looked to see Frank standing there then he said, "How's that for cold water, Lou?"

My reply to him was, "You did not just throw that glass of water on me, Frank Henderson! The water fight is on Mister!"

Quickly, I ran to the back door but Frank was already running out our front door. Grabbing a bucket off the shelf in the washroom, I filled it with water at the sink then went in pursuit of my laughing husband. Evidently, Frank thought I would follow him out the front door but that was not my plan. Hearing him coming around to the back of the house, I ducked down in the kitchen so he could not see me as he passed the kitchen window.

When Frank entered the back door, I drenched him with my bucket of water then ran out the front door. Frank started chasing me around the house but suddenly he was not behind me. After trying to open the front, I discovered it was locked, so I tried the back door which was also locked. Knowing Frank so well, I knew he was up to something, so I decided to go to our good friends who lived next door for some backup troops.

As I walked up to knock on their door, the door suddenly opened, and they pulled me inside their house. They had been watching the whole "Frank and Nancy Water Fight" from their bedroom window. They were more than willing to help me, so we made a plan of attack. Their baby boy was down for a nap and we agreed that we were all responsible to check on him.

Frank's buddy would go to the door of our house, knock, get Frank to open the door then my girlfriend and I standing out of Frank's site would soak him with two huge pitchers of water. Secretly my girlfriend and I had made another plan which did not include her husband hearing or needing to know. When the husband went to our door and knocked on the door, Frank answered the door then opened it widely he said, "Hurry up and come in. I know Nancy is hiding out there."

Suddenly two pitchers full of water were thrown at those two soldiers standing at the doorway. My girlfriend and I got them both then we ran. Now we had established teams but there were no rules except making sure baby boy was checked on, britches changed, and not harmed in any way. You just never knew when you would get soaked. Going to a window to look outside became an instant soaking from some thrown water.

Since both houses had tile floors, while we ran through the houses chasing each other, we were slip-sliding away, busting it on the floors, getting back up, laughing loudly, then going to the sinks to get more water to throw. This went on for about an hour and it was absolutely priceless. When we called a truce, our floors in our homes were mostly all very wet except for baby boy's bedroom because his room was a safehouse or a hideout.

All of us helped clean up the water then we decided to cook hamburgers, hang out at our house, and listen to music. Frank and I had a way of being contagious and spreading our playfulness between the two of us to others. Thinking God had a lot to do with that.

Not too long after the Water Fight, Frank came home telling me that it was required that I attend a meeting on Torri Station for all wives of ASA soldiers. Being curious as to what this meeting was all about, I agreed to go.

After arriving at the meeting then being seated, soon we were given a presentation or should I say a demand then handed a piece of paper. Seems the new requirement for wives of ASA soldiers was to sign a piece of paper that stated if we heard our husbands talking in their sleep or if they talked to us about top secret stuff that we would turn them into their superiors.

For some reason, this made me instantly furious. I got up to leave and while walking to the door was halted by a man in uniform then told I needed to sign the paper then turn it in. Well now, I just handed him the paper, told him no and walked out the door.

That afternoon, Frank came in with that piece of paper in his hand, looked at me smiling, then said, "Nancy, I need you to sign this piece of paper."

I told him, "Frank, I am not signing a piece of paper telling me to rat on my husband. You do not talk in your sleep. You do not tell me about your work. Sorry, but if you want that piece of paper signed, you will have to sign my name on it. I am not in the Army because they didn't issue me a uniform."

Frank started laughing as he signed my name on the paper then he grabbed me in his arms, told me he loved me then kissed me. You know what? He didn't do half-bad signing my name.

The evening shift would prove to be a hard one for Frank, especially when it was his last one to work after twenty-nine of them.

Since we were just across the street from Torii Station, Frank would often walk to work leaving me the car in case I needed it to go somewhere. Frank had done just that on his last evening shift that afternoon. After Frank left for work, I cleaned the house, washed then hung out clothes, and later made a special supper for him to have when he got home late that night.

Since the evening was still young, I decided to start reading a new book that I had purchased at the PX on base. It was a long book called Airport written by Arthur Hailey. It did not take long for me to get totally absorbed in reading this book. After a while, I checked the time then realize that Frank would be coming in the door very soon, so I turned the oven on warm, covered the food I had made with foil (Texan fall) then placed it in the oven to warm.

About 12:00 a.m., I realized where Frank was and he had forgotten about the "silent treatment." I decided to write a note to put on the front door. This note simply read

> *FRANK,*
> *YOU ARE A BIG BOY. BUT IF YOU CAN'T*
> *LET ME KNOW WHERE YOU ARE OR COME*
> *HOME ON TIME, YOU CAN SLEEP OUTSIDE*
> *WITH RALPH. SLEEP WELL, DIMPLES.*
> *I LOVE YOU VERY MUCH,*
> *NANCY LOU*

Soon I heard a singing very drunk Frank coming up to the door. There was a pause as he read the note then he knocked on the door saying, "I'm sorry. Please, let me in Nancy."

I did not respond to him but I heard him sit down on the porch then tell Ralph, "I really messed up Ralph. I was just gonna have one beer but then I drank many more. Guess you and I are gonna be out here tonight."

After sitting back down on the couch while trying to decide how long I would let him stay outside side, I heard Frank get up then walk — stumble — around the side of the house heading to the back door. Realizing that the back door might not be locked, I ran to the back door and locked it just as he got to it. He heard me so he knocked on the back door but I did not respond.

Suddenly, I heard a sound coming from our bedroom, so I ran to the bedroom. The bedroom window was open with a box fan sitting on the ledge which was our "Okinawa air-conditioner." Frank was working on pulling the wooden stealy bars off the outside of the window when ran to the window, grabbed the fan out of it then slammed it closed and locked it. Frank and I started laughing loudly staring at each other through the window.

Realizing he had exhausted all ways to get into the house, Frank turned from the window then walked back to the front yard and sat down on the porch with Ralph. After he had been sitting there for a few minutes, I went to the front door then asked him through the closed door, "Do you think you can be a good boy for a while now?

Frank responded, "Yes, Nancy Lou."

I opened the door then let Frank come into the house. He was shaking his head while smiling at me and saying, "I love you, Nancy Lou."

Frank sat down then I fixed him a plate of the warm food that was in the oven. He ate his food then we went to bed and he was a good boy the rest of the night since he fell sound asleep when his head touched the pillow

Of course, I could never be sure of what might happen the next day but that would take all of the fun out of loving him just the way he was. The most important thing for me was to not change him but to totally love him.

We were twenty years old, totally in love with each other, and enjoying every moment of it. We were slip-sliding away into becoming one soul and heart bound to each other for eternity.

39

roller coaster

Beginning of the summer of 1970, we had settled into our daily lives in Okinawa. We were enjoying every moment together, but soon things would disrupt that peace sending us on a roller coaster of emotions.

Since Frank was on the day shift, I was surprised when he came home at lunchtime one day. Visibly upset as he entered the house he asked me to sit down, which I immediately did.

With tears in his eyes, Frank said, "Nancy, I need you to pack a bag because I need you to go home."

Being so in tune with Frank's heart and soul, I knew that there was something wrong which he could not tell me. Also, I knew that there was no way that I was going home and leave him alone.

While looking into his eyes and seeing the emotion in them, I replied, "Frank, I am not going home no matter what."

Tears rolled slowly from Frank's eyes as he said, "Nancy, I love so much, I need you out of harm's way, and I can't tell you any more than that."

Well, he really didn't need to say more because whatever was upsetting him about my safety meant he was not safe either. There was no way was I ever going to leave him in Okinawa alone.

I told him, "Frank, I am not going home no matter what. Whatever comes our way we will be here together to face it. I love you and we are one. I can't leave you."

Frank held me tightly for a long time as I gently rubbed his head then we kissed and he went back to Torii Station but before leaving he told me that he would have to stay on the base and work round the clock for a few days. A couple of days later, Frank came in smiling and I knew the threat was finally over.

Frank's job with the ASA meant he would have access to sensitive material. I know that Cambodia, Russia, China,

Japan, and Vietnam were part of the concerns during the time we were on Okinawa.

There were many riots happening in Okinawa in 1969-1970. Frank and I had witnessed one of these riots when we lived a couple of blocks from Kadena Circle. Riot police from Japan marched down the street in block formation in front of our home clubbing Okinawans who did not disperse quickly.

Supposedly, these riots by Okinawans were for the Ryukyu Islands return to Japan and the removal of the B-52s on Kadena Air Base but if you talked to Okinawans they did not want anything to do with going back to Japan. There was also a rumor Japan had a submarine circling the Island.

After things calmed down, Frank decided to put in for an extension of his tour in Okinawa. Staying on the Island for another year would mean that most likely Frank would make Sp5 which would mean we would get to send all of our possessions and pets home free. Also, I would get to fly home free with Frank. It also meant that Frank would end his enlistment to the ASA in Okinawa. It seemed our roller coaster of emotions was climbing to new heights of bliss for us.

A few weeks later, when I went to hang out clothes on the clothesline, Ralph was by my side. Ralph always followed us everywhere we went. He would sit patiently in the driveway with me by his side as we waited for Frank to walk across the street.

After the clothes were all hung on the clothesline, I went back into the house then looking at the clock noticed it was time for Frank to come in from work. Thinking Ralph had followed me into the house, I called his name but he did not come to me. Suddenly realizing he had not followed me inside, I ran to the front screen door but as I opened it there was a screeching of brakes followed by a loud thud. My heart sank.

After running to the driveway, I saw Frank in the middle of the road picking up, Ralph. As Frank walked towards me with Ralph in his arms, tears were streaming down his face. I could not get my breath, tears flooded from my eyes as I ran to Frank. We did not speak as we sat down on our porch together while Frank held Ralph's lifeless body in his lap. Our roller coaster of emotions had just taken a sharp drop heading downhill.

Frank and I buried our sweet Ralph together, shed more tears then Frank broke the silence with tears running down his face saying, "Nancy, I am so sorry, Ralph saw me on the other side of the road then ran to me. He didn't see the car coming."

Trying to hold back my own tears, I told him, "No, Frank it is not your fault. It's mine. I thought he was inside with me but he didn't follow me into the house from the clothesline. I am so sorry."

We held each other tightly that evening and night then the next morning we made Ralph a cross for his grave. As the weeks passed the pain and heartache would become more bearable but neither one of us would ever forget our Ralph. The roller coaster of emotions had nowhere to go but up.

After a couple of months passed, we decided that since Frank had not yet heard from his extension to stay on Okinawa, that it was definitely going to go through. I bought some nice drapery material, borrowed a sewing machine from a girlfriend then made draperies for our living room. Also, Frank and I bought a two-tier table to go into the living room. The roller coaster of emotions was climbing the hill to blissfulness again.

One afternoon when Frank in from work, he had our friends from next door with him. I laughed asking him if we were going to have a party but he was not smiling when he asked me to sit down. I sat down on the couch and my girl-friend sat down close to me.

Frank looked at his buddy standing by his side then he squatted down in front of me, took my hands into his, then looked into my eyes as he told me, "Nancy, I did not get an extension. I will be going to Vietnam. They called three of us into an office at work then told us one of us would have to go to Vietnam because they only had two extensions then they told us to decide. I volunteered to go. The other two men and their wives have children. They are close friends of ours, each family has three children, and one man's wife is pregnant. Nancy, I love you, I know your heart, and I know you will understand and will agree with my decision."

Looking into Frank's eyes, I tried to process what he had just told me. My heart was so proud of him but in the pit of my stomach, it felt like a knife had pierced me. Waves of fear began to overtake me and my body began to shake but I continued to look steadily into his eyes.

My mind went to our friends and their families that Frank had spoken of then I replied, "Frank, I am so proud of you and I love you so much. I understand your heart and soul. I totally agree with your decision."

Our friends left our home so we could be alone. Frank and I talked for hours about everything. Frank told me that they promised to up his rank to SP5 which meant we could ship our possessions home free and we would not have to pay for my ticket home. Also, we decide on how and when to tell our parents. After we went to bed, we held each other tightly all night long.

The roller coaster made of emotions had just gone over the top of the hill heading towards a very close fork in the rails which would try to separate our joined emotions by putting them on two different rails but we knew in our hearts that we had one heart and soul which was inseparably and headed to a future of being an even stronger one body of emotions traveling together for eternity.

Frank would not get his promotion to SP5. It seems they had misplaced the paperwork or had forgotten to put him in for the promotion, either way, he was furious.

Since we were allowed to ship only 200-lbs home free, we sold all of our furniture but we did pay to ship our stereo equipment home. We decided to save $50 on my ticket home by getting a more economical flight which we were told would not include me flying on a new plane called a 747. We specifically asked because I did not want to fly on one of those huge planes.

Frank surprised me by telling me he had decided to ship our cats, Candy and Homer, home. I was thrilled. We actually sold our car, Ole Bondo, for what we paid for it. Frank and I were so busy that we didn't have time to think about what the future held for us which was a good thing.

My flight had a set date that I would leave Okinawa. Frank had to take a Forty-five day leave just to go home to see his folks and get me settled in because Vietnam was a direct transfer from Okinawa and the Army would not pay for him to go home to the states but he could catch a hop on a military plane to get home.

This meant we would have to go to the base in the evening to wait until he got a flight out. If he did not get put on a flight that first evening then the procedure would be repeated every evening until he did.

We decided to start the evening trip to Kadena Air Base two days before my flight was to leave. We really thought it could take days for Frank to get on a flight out. Much to our surprise, the first evening he got on a flight to the states which left me in Okinawa alone.

We knew that this was a possibility, so we had made plans for me to stay with our next door neighbors and friends. Needless to say, my folks were not really pleased when Frank got home, went to see them, then told them I was still in Okinawa. Oh, to have been a fly on that wall!

My economical flight home proved to be quite the learning experience. Once the plane took off from Naha Airport, we flew to Saipan then landed on a dirt runway sitting next to what looked like a hut where we picked up two new passengers then took flight again.

Next stop was Guam where I had a two-hour layover and where I met some other women in the waiting room traveling to the states. We all loaded onto a different plane that took off very fast down a short runway ending at the edge of a cliff. The plane actually dipped down as it left the runway then flew upward. I think they called that flight "sink or fly" but not sure.

The next stop was Honolulu, a beautiful airport. We all had to go through customs there and for some reason, the officials chose me to get to have my suitcases rummaged through while I stood there and watched but by this time I really cared less.

After the rummage party, I met up with my new friends who were talking to a young soldier who was headed home to the states. He asked us if he could buy us all a drink in the lobby bar. Since we had a layover of about four hours, we decided that we would let him buy us that drink. Of course, we were totting all of our luggage which had to be checked in at the next gate.

As you all know, my experience with alcohol is not good, so I ordered what was called a Mai Tai. This drink was full of big chunks of pineapple, had an orange slice, then a cherry on top. It even had a little umbrella sticking out of one of the pieces of pineapple. I drank it all down then ate all of the fruit. When we got up to leave, it was all I could do to drag my biggest suitcase.

Our next flight boarded on the second floor, so after we climbed the stairs then all staggered to the second-floor gate, and checked in our luggage, we just waited in the lobby until time to load onto the plane. The lobby had huge windows to look out of. I noticed a huge plane sitting next to the window being worked but I knew it was not my plane because I was not flying on a 747. I was so wrong.

After loading onto the 747 the next stop was Los Angeles. You could barely see the lights because a brown smog covered the town that night but we landed safely. I had to catch a taxi to a different terminal where I would find my next gate to load on another plane to fly to Texas.

After getting to the terminal, finding my gate, and knowing there was a six-hour layover, I decided to find the closest phone booth to make a call home. After flying up and down for nearly a full day, I was exhausted. Frank answered his parent's phone and it was so good to hear his voice. We couldn't talk very long because it was a long distance call but we talked long enough to renew my strength.

Finally, the layover ended then I loaded on to the last plane which would be flying me to Texas. The plane was fairly full of people but as we landed in different towns, Las Vegas, El Paso, and San Antonio, letting off passengers before taking flight again, it ended up that just the pilot, co-pilot, stewardess, a guy and I were the only passengers left to get off in Houston. Glad I didn't know we were going to do that.

Early in the morning, Frank and Jimmy picked me up at the new airport in Houston. Once stepping off the plane at Houston Intercontinental Airport, I discovered it had been

36 hours since I had left Okinawa. My "economical" flight was so much fun.

Frank and I only had forty-five days together before he would leave to go back to Okinawa for two weeks then be transferred to Vietnam.

40

broken hearts

After nearly two years of living together in Okinawa, late November 1970, Frank and I returned to Van Vleck, Texas.

We tried not to think about the short time we had left together but it was always in the back of our minds. In less than forty-five days, Frank would fly back to Okinawa for two weeks then transfer to Vietnam.

Before leaving Okinawa, Frank and I had sat down and made plans for what we wanted to do when we got home. We wanted to have a place of our own where we could spend time alone together before he left for Vietnam. It was also very important for us to have memories of living in this new home together and be able to picture each other there together.

Frank knew that I was a very private person when it came to displaying deep emotions. He wanted me to have a place to go and be alone with my emotions privately. So Frank and I rented a little white house in Van Vleck.

Not having any furniture to furnish this new home, thanks to our parents, we quickly acquired some. We were given a couch, a chair, and my antique bedroom set (you might remember this bed from another chapter). Since the house was furnished with a stove and refrigerator, we did not have to buy those two appliances. We had stored most of our things at Frank's Folk's home before we went to Okinawa, so we had everything else we needed.

Frank and I had decided in Okinawa that we would need a car and what kind of car we wanted to buy. We bought a new Volkswagen Super Beetle in Freeport, Texas a few days after arriving home. I was going to apply for a job and work while Frank was in Vietnam. We would need a vehicle to drive while Frank was on leave and for me to drive while he was in Vietnam.

After settling into our new home, Candy and Homer, our cats, finally arrived in Houston but had to be quarantined. Finally, Frank and I went to pick them up. They had been quarantined for two weeks before we could get them and they were as happy to see us as we were to see them. Our small family was finally all together again.

Christmas and all of the beauty of what it means came. Frank and I bought a Christmas tree and decorated it with lights, ornaments, and silver colored icicles. Candy and Homer did their best to climb the tree and bat off the ornaments but we didn't mind. We laid close to each other on a plush rug on the floor while listening to music on our Reel to Reel that we had shipped home before we left Okinawa. All seemed peaceful in the world but the days were passing by way too quickly.

Christmas came and went then it was January of 1971. Frank and I celebrated the New Year together but we knew that time was growing short until he would have to leave on a flight back to Okinawa. There was so much we wanted and needed to say to each other and we talked a lot but not about how to say goodbye. The thought of being separated from each other for a year without knowing what the future held for us was totally overwhelming and we just chose to not talk about it.

On January 7, 1971, Frank and I were driven to the Airport in Houston by family. We rode together in the back seat of one of the cars. We were lost in our own world, sitting as close to each other as we could, holding each other, saying "I love you", staring into each other's eyes, and trying to memorize each other's faces.

Once we got to the terminal where Frank would load the plane for his flight, I can remember feeling weak in the knees and trembling. Frank checked in his duffel bag then we went to the gate where he would board his plane. It was not long until his flight number was called and it was time for us to say goodbye before he would board his plane and my heart felt like it stopped.

Frank and I embraced each other tightly, looked into each other's eyes while saying "I love you" then we kissed. We tried to be strong for each other but nothing could have prepared us for our goodbye. After the second call came to load the plane, Frank released his arms from around me then walked toward the gate but turned around at the entrance to the tunnel to wave goodbye then saw me standing there in tears.

Frank had tears in his eyes as he quickly walked back to me, hugged me, kissed me as he wiped away my tears while telling me how much he loved me. My heart was breaking and I could not breathe much less speak but as Frank turned to walk back to the gate, I ran after him, embraced him telling him how much I loved him then we kissed one more time not wanting to ever end our embrace.

The gate person came to Frank and told him that he must load the plane, then he gently took Frank's arm leading him away from me. I watched Frank walk down the tunnel then disappear as he loaded onto the plane. One of our family members gently guided me away from the gate to the windows where I stood and watched Frank's plane leave.

My mind kept thinking, "How can I survive if something happens to him? He is my heart and soul." Suddenly, while standing there watching his plane taxi down the runway and take flight, I stopped crying, felt a sudden warmth and a growing strength inside me, I realized God was standing by my side reassuring me and comforting me.

Once Frank's plane was out of site, we all left the airport then headed back to Van Vleck. There was not a lot of talking in the car as we made our way back to Frank's folk's home.

Our car was left at their home, so I started to get in it to head to our little white house but they wanted me to come inside to visit and asked if I wanted to spend the night. Since it was getting dark and I really did not want to go home alone to an empty house, I agreed to stay.

About midnight, Frank's folk's phone rang. It was Frank calling from the Airport in Houston. He had gotten off the plane in San Antonio, had flown back to Houston, and needed someone to come pick him up. Frank's Dad and I got into his folk's car then headed to Houston to the airport. Frank was waiting outside the terminal by the drive-through drop off when we got there. Once we stopped the car he put his duffel bag into the trunk, got into the car, and we headed back to Van Vleck.

After Frank got into the car and we were headed back to Van Vleck, I asked him, "Frank, what happened? What are you doing?"

Frank answered, "Nancy, I wasn't ready to leave you yet, so I turned around and came back."

When we got to Frank's folk's house, Frank and I got into our car then drove to our little white house. We spent all night together talking, crying, praying, and just holding each other tightly then when morning came we returned to the airport in Houston.

Once Frank and I got to the gate to say goodbye, we were strong for each other, we smiled at each other, and gave each other the most beautiful goodbye without tears but with renewed hope in the strength and love that God had given us through our prayers. We knew that being separated would never pull us apart because our true love for each other was inseparable. We were of one heart and soul.

Frank was ten hours late getting back to Okinawa then to Torii Station but I'll let him tell you about it.

January 8-9, 1971
Dear Nancy,

Well, I got into Naha at 9:00 a.m. this morning (8th). By the time I got signed in it was 10:00 a.m. and I was 10 hours late. But I got in no serious trouble. It was a long flight as you well know.

Our friends invited me over for supper. I'm now sitting at work and it's 5:45 a.m. in the morning. Tomorrow is my last working day. My plane leaves for Saigon at 0950 (9:50 a.m.) on the 16th and I get there at 1640 (4:40 p.m.).

All I can think of is how much I miss you and love you. But when I get to feeling too depressed, I think about a day about a year from now when we will meet in Oakland and never have to lose sight of one another again. That makes me happy. Very happy. Think about it. I'm sure it'll make you feel better also.

I'm going to have to close for now. I'll write a little more some other time. Because I have to get to work or else I'm in trouble. I just wanted you to know I arrived safely and how much I love and miss you. Say hi to everyone.

Sorry about my writing but I'm hurrying before the E-6 gets back. See you soon and keep loving me as you always have. I love you dearly.

Yours forever,
Frank
P.S. 372 DLITA (Days Left In The Army)

Frank was struggling once getting back to Okinawa without me. We had lived together there for nearly two years. Our friends were trying to help him out with his loneliness but they lived right next door to the house Frank and I had lived in and moved from forty-five days before. I know that each time Frank saw the home we had shared in Okinawa it played on his heart.

The next letter was written on the back of the one above.

January 10, 1971,
Dear Nancy,
Hi again. I hope this day finds you well and happy. Well, I went red Sunday morning at 7:30 a.m. (today). Everyone misses you and asks how you are. I stay in the barracks all my time except to go to our friend's house when they invite me.

I've been to the club first time today at 8:00 a.m. after we got off work and ate breakfast (35 cents) and I haven't had a beer yet. So see there is no need to worry about me.

Nancy, you're the only one in my life and I'm happy with the way things are. I need no one else to comfort me or to think about me but you. Why is it I finally find the one thing I've dreamed about and thought about and wanted all my life and have to leave it? But when this year is up I'll never leave it again. You're the most IMPORTANT thing in my whole life.

It feels good to have a love for someone like the love I have for you. I pray for your safety and happiness and for the love we both share. I remember my old graduation theme, "With God for us who can be against us". I close with that and all my love for as long as my body continues to breathe.

Your Loving Husband,
Frank

It took at least five days for a letter to get from the states to Okinawa. So, a letter written to someone asking them a question would take at least ten days for you to get that answer. Snail mail was slow but it was the only form of communication we had. No email. No Skype. No cellphones. The only other choice we had was communication through shortwave radio operators which included a long distance call. Of course, that would not be an option once Frank got to Vietnam.

January 12, 1971
Dearest Nancy,

Hello, my love. Hello, my wife. Hello, my lover. I say hello to you. I got your letter today and I believe it was the nicest thing that has happened to me this week. You know how to say the right things to me.

You know I can't visualize life without you. Not the fact that I'm going to be away from you but the fact that I can't remember what life was like without you before you came into my life and how life would be now without you. After loving you and knowing you, life wouldn't be worth living without you by my side.

People say God has a purpose for everyone and I sincerely believe my purpose is to love you and make a happy home for you and our children. I want nothing more from life. The world can have their ulcers, diseases, pollutions, money worries and societies. I need none of these. What I need is what I got, a good faithful loving wife who cares only for me. What more could I want? My cup runneth over.

I really feel I'm the luckiest person alive. I'm dead serious. Sometimes I believe my heart could burst with love for you. I know you're lonely but so am I. But why should we be? I have enough love in my heart for you that ought to carry me through a year. How about you?

Hey beautiful, I love you. Let's each night say a prayer for each other and tell each other we love each other. Nancy, we're strong together. Our love is too strong to ever fade and die. I have to go now. Just never forget that I love you so much and will also do so.

So goodnight for now and my God watch over you. All my love for you and you alone.

Your Faithful Husband,

Frank

P.S. 368 DLITA

P.S.P.S. California here we come.

Frank had gotten his first letter from me and he was so happy. Frank and I loved God as much as He loved us. Vietnam would be the hardest thing that we would face together as a married couple but our true love for each other would only be strengthened by the very thing that tried to separate us.

Frank and I were only twenty-one years old but our true love for each other and our love for God would make us the strongest of love warriors even though we were separated by thousands of miles and an ocean. Love like ours could not be separated. We were of one heart and soul.

41

last letters

Frank was trying to deal with his loneliness in Okinawa while I was dealing with that same loneliness in Van Vleck. Handwritten letters were our way of communicating our feelings to each other.

After Frank returned to the island for a short time before being sent to Vietnam, I could see in my mind where he was living and working which gave me so much comfort. We had lived across the road from Torii Station and had been on the base many times, so I knew it very well.

Since we had rented the little white house in Van Vleck once arriving home from Okinawa, Frank could envision me in our little home which would prove to be a very stabling factor for his emotions. He needed to be able to close his eyes and see me in our home. We thought Frank would be in Okinawa for two weeks before his transfer to Vietnam but that proved not to be true. He would end up leaving for Vietnam only eight days after he returned to Okinawa. Neither one of us was prepared for that to happen so soon.

These are the last letters I received from Frank before he left for Vietnam and a letter I sent to him that was returned to me because it did not arrive before he left Okinawa.

> *January 14, 1971 10:00 p.m.*
> *Dear Nancy,*
> *Hello Darling. How's everything with you? I'm almost through clearing post. I'll finish up in the morning. I'll be gone by the time you get this letter.*
> *Our friends had a 9lb. 6oz. baby boy. They seem really happy about it. There's not too much to say about this place.*
> *It's the same old place. Except for one thing. There's an ugly freckled faced man living in the barracks. I don't think he belongs there because he doesn't fit in. He just*

lays around reads and mopes. He looks like he's very lonely and misses someone very much. He keeps mumbling about the Army and how bad he hates it and how in 366 days he's going to meet someone in California and have a wonderful time.

No. Seriously. Honey, I'm looking forward to that day so much. Don't worry about me. Sure I'm lonely and miss you but I'll make it. And the reason I'll make it is because I have your love to fall back on and that love is so strong it'll carry me through anything.

You don't have to worry about me, Honey. I'll be faithful to you, I swear. What do I need another woman for? Your love is too strongly impressed on my memory and my heart to even think about it. So don't waste your time worrying about that. If you must worry, worry about how you're going to take care of all those kids we're going to have. Would you be disappointed if we only had 16?

Darling, I love you. You know that? Well, you'd better. Say hello to everyone and tell them I'm doing fine and tell them and the whole world how much I Love You.

Well, time to get some crash time in. Do you still love me? Give me a kiss good-night and say a prayer for me and tell me you love me and I'll see you soon.

Your faithful loving husband,
Frank
P.S. Our friends say to write.
P.S.P.S. I love you very much

The loneliness and uncertainty of things to come were beginning to play on Frank's mind. He knew how much I trusted him and loved him but he needed to reassure me of his faithfulness and love for me. I never once doubted Frank's faithfulness to me in our entire married life.

After arriving in Okinawa to live with Frank, a single GI was visiting in our home and helping me in the kitchen while I was washing dishes. He told me that my Frank was one of the only married men, that he knew who would not go to bars and had not participated in extracurricular activities with pay for women. Of course, he did not have to tell me that but he said he wanted me to know how much Frank loved me. I can still see this young man's face as he told me this even now and it is a priceless memory.

Frank's thoughts and emotions continued to confuse him as he writes this next letter. He was so worried about me but my only thought was how much I loved him and my only concerns were about his safety and survival.

In this letter, Frank's handwriting changes from his previous letter and you can see him try to talk to me while he tried to fight the emotions he was feeling.

> *January 15, 1971 11:40 a.m.*
> *Dear Nancy,*
> *Well, I'm through clearing. I'm just waiting to leave. You know how much I hated this place and couldn't wait to leave, well now it's no big deal. I miss you here just like I will in Nam.*
>
> *That 45 days we had meant so much to me. So much, that now I can see how great it's going to be when we get out. All the worries we'll have will seem so petty after having been through all the things we've had to face together. And we pulled through all of them. And we'll keep right on pulling through them.*
>
> *We're a team. At times it felt like it was you and me against the whole world. We may have faltered but we never fell. We need to lean on each other when things get bad. Here I am spouting off about "we" and it's me doing*

all the talking. I hope you feel the same about me and the things I think about as I do about you.

How's everything at home? I worry a lot about you. Please keep me informed about your emotions, your loneliness, and all your feelings. I know this is silly and stupid of me and you'll probably get mad at me for this but I worry about you being lonely and needing comforting in your loneliness and seek someone else.

Now I don't mean you'd intentionally do this but unintentionally. It happens. God knows I trust you but that doesn't keep me from worrying. Women need someone to lean on and I'm not there for you to lean on. I'm not accusing you or believing that you'd do it.

Oh hell. I don't know what I'm even thinking. All I know is that I couldn't stand being without you. I love you and need you to be my wife. I'm sorry if anything I said offended you or made you mad. Please realize I didn't mean anything by it or anything else. Sometimes something bothers me and it obsesses my mind.

I have no doubts about you. I trust you, respect you, and love you. Why I get this way I don't know. It's just one of my many faults I guess. Do you sometimes worry about me? If you do, please tell me. I'm just asking you to forgive me for my stupidness. I'm sorry.

Nancy, I don't know what to say to you. I can't express or explain the knot in my stomach when I hear a song we both liked or think of you. I'm not good at expressing myself on paper. All I can say is I love you and hope that you get the message out of this.

Your loving husband,
Frank
P.S. Tell the animals hi.

Reading this letter now versus reading it so many years ago, I see so much pain going through Frank's heart. His fear of losing me was deeper than his fear of going to Vietnam. He knew how much I loved him but his emotions were not letting him think clearly.

The next thing that he would have to face was not being able to get mail from me. The last letter I wrote to Frank while he was in Okinawa was written on January 11, 1971. He did not receive this letter because by the time it arrived he had already departed for Vietnam.

> *January 11, 1971*
> *Dear Frank,*
> *Well hello. How's my favorite guy? I hope fine. If you haven't guessed by now, I am practicing typing. I am afraid I am not doing to good. I am pretty sure, I am going to be working at the Credit Bureau as a clerk typist. Ha! Ha! That is why I am practicing typing. I think my future is pretty dim. In a minute, I am going to try to type a sentence without any errors. (That will be the day)*
> *Well, how is it with you. I hope fine. I am fine, except for missing you. I am already planning for our second honeymoon. I can hardly wait until we are together again. You just wait, I am going to Love You to death! I love you too much for your own good. I love you, Frank!*
> *I thought I would get a letter from you today, but I guess you have been busy. Have you started to process out yet? I hope you are eating right because I would die if you got sick. I love you, Frank!*
> *Have you seen our friends since you have been back? Has their baby boy grown much? I bet he has really grown and is really cute.*

Frank as soon as you get your W2 form please send it to me. If you will, I can go ahead and send off our Income Tax form and get that money back so I can send you some money. I know you are broke and need money. I wish I had the money to send it to you now but I can't spare a red cent because of the car payments.

I had the car checked last Friday at the Volkswagen place in Freeport and they said it was alright. Your Dad went with me. I wanted to get it checked before I started to work, so I did.

Frank, I want you to know I love you and need you very much. I pray the time will pass by quickly and bring you home to me very soon. Please take care of yourself and be careful because you have a wife so very much in love with you and who needs you very much.

I'll close for now but I'll write you again tomorrow. I LOVE YOU!!!!!

ALL MY LOVE TO YOU MY DARLING,
I Love You,
Nancy

In the letter above, you will notice that I had not gotten letters from Frank yet. It would be at least January 13 of 14, 1971 before I would get his first letters but I kept writing.

Once Frank got to Vietnam, he would not have an address for me to write to him for a while but he would keep writing to me and I continued to write to him every day saving the letters to mail when I got his address.

I pray you have gotten to know Frank and me because there are many beautiful letters to come. We shared a true soulmate love for each other. We were one heart and soul which could not be separated by the separation of war.

Stay Tuned!

Nancy Lou Henderson writes. A lot. Some of the items she writes are funny and irreverent. Other pieces are introspective and thought-provoking. And let's not even get started on the ones that will make you a blubbering mess because they are so heart-wrenching and poignant.

That's why you have to *stay tuned*!
Connect with Nancy.
Follow her blog.
Find her on Facebook.
Tweet her on Twitter.
Use these links to connect.

Ⓦ *www.nancylouhenderson.com*

🅕 facebook.com/nancy.henderson.39

🐦 @nlhende49

Please help us bring awareness to Nancy's work. Tell everyone you know how much you enjoyed this book. Ask your local bookstore to stock it. And please-please-please give it a good review on Amazon. It's kind gestures like these that help Nancy and other independent authors to carry on bringing you such wonderful and heart-felt work for your enjoyment and edification. Thank you!

A *Very Special Preview of War & Commitment: The Love Story of Nancy & Frank: Book II*

1

waiting on an address

Frank deployed from Okinawa to Vietnam on January 15, 1971. I would not receive the last letter he wrote from Okinawa until after he had been deployed for five days.

One of the letters I had written to him dated January 11, 1971, was returned to me. Because I wrote him a letter every day, I know somewhere out there in "lost letter land" there are still other letters that he never received and which were never returned to me. The problem we faced was that mail took five days or more to arrive in Okinawa from the states.

The following letter is the first letter I received from Frank while he was in Vietnam.

January 19, 1971
Dear Lou,

Well, how's it been? I got here at 3:30 p.m. in the afternoon from Kadena after stopping at Taiwan and the Philippines. Tomorrow is my 5th day at the Trans. Co. at the 509th. The first day, Saturday, I got here too late to do anything. The next day, Sunday, I had to go to Long Binh (90th) to get my jungle fatigues, boots, helmet, and get this green shorts, green t-shirts, green towels, and handkerchiefs. Boy,,am I, ever "green". I look like a real trooper. Funny thing is I don't feel like one.

I'm sorry I haven't written before this but ever since Monday, I've pulled detail every day from 7:30 a.m. to about 6:00 p.m. then I have to hustle to eat. A quick shower and a cigarette then crash-time. Also, I didn't want to write you until I get a permanent-place so you could write back. You can't write here because they said it would take 3 weeks for them to find us after we left. And by the time you get this letter, I'll probably (better be) be gone to my permanent station.

Sorry, I had to do something about that damn spider. I bet I knock that same one off of the rafter over my bunk every night. I don't think I'll ever get used to sleeping on a narrow cot by myself. I'm used to having that warm soft body next to me that belongs to my wife.

Nancy, I'm sorry once again about that letter I sent. I have a lot of frustrations and anxieties running around in my head. I'm confused and mixed up. I have a lot of soul searching to do and it needs doing. I've got to find out what kind of person I am. I want to be a new and different kind of person for you. I've come to believe I've been wrong by you and I've done you wrong in the past and now if it's not late, I want to make up these discrepancies to you.

When I leave this country, I want to be the right kind of husband and father. We have, I believe, the basic requirements for a happy marriage; love and youthfulness. With a little refinement on my part, it can be twice what it's been. I don't want to disappoint you once or make you unhappy. Darling, I want so much to make you happy and I'm going to I promise.

Has Ebony had her puppies yet? How're the cats? And how's our new SUPER BEETLE? Our friends in Okinawa want on so bad they can taste it. Tell everyone that I'll write when I get to wherever it is, I'm going.

Darling don't worry about me. So far everything is ok. Except, I miss you too much already. Also, it's too hot to believe and at night I wake up cold. But every day I wake up brings me closer to you. I don't start out every day sad and depressed. That one thought gets me to the day's end and then I think, well when I go to sleep, I'll wake up a day shorter toward being in your arms again. Boy, it makes time pass fast. I've been here for four days already and it doesn't seem like it's been only 4 years. HA! HA! Joke. Joke.

All jokes and my faults out of the way. I love you, Nancy. I write that, but it seems so small. It means so much, but 4 words take care of it. It's a shame I can't record my thoughts maybe they would convey the way I feel about you. I'll let you know in 361 days.

Anyway, I do love you and miss you. I'll write when I get a new address. Till then remember me in your prayers and know in your heart I love you.

Your husband,
Frank
P.S. Tell everyone hello.
P.S.P.S. Here's some of our money. MPC.

Frank was waiting to get to his final destination in Vietnam. He was still trying to get his thoughts together. The last letter Frank received from me had to have been written on January 9, 1971, and he would have received it on January 15, 1971.

Frank was lonely and missed me. I was lonely and missed him. Frank knew he would not start receiving letters from me until he got an address but after he mailed me the address it would take ten days from that day for him to get a letter from me. It took five days for me to receive his mail then five days for a letter from me to get back to him.

I got the job at the Credit Bureau in Bay City, Texas which with my typing "talents," was a true miracle. My day consisted of getting up, getting dressed, going to work, working, coming home, feeding the animals, maybe eating supper, getting ready for bed, crying, and writing Frank a letter. Nights were the worst time for me.

Frank was beginning to adjust and accept being in Vietnam so much more in this next letter.

> *January 25, 1971*
> *Dear Nancy,*
> *Well, here I am again. I'm sorry it's been so long between writings, but I got stuck at the 509th for 7 days because I couldn't get my orders. I got to the 8th RRFS on the 22nd. I processed for 2 days and today (Monday, 25th) I started a kind of orientation. Neat stuff like firing the M-16, M-79, M-60, gas mask and other bullshit I've had in Devens and Okinawa. I had an E-7 instructor ask me today if I learned anything yet and I said, "Hell No, I've had this training twice before.*
> *I got my address yesterday, but this is the first time I've had time to write. They keep you busy around here if you're not working in Ops. Guess who I saw 5 minutes*

after I got here? Lee, he thought we were gone when he came to Okie (Okinawa) on leave.

You know that last letter I wrote to you must have been a pain to read. I guess I sounded like an 18-year-old kid. If I did, I apologize for it. I've found my strength again. I'm facing reality now and I believe I've found the real me again. Like I promised you. I've thought quite a bit about how a good husband should, be and these many hours of thought brought me out of my doubts in myself and my doubts and illusions about life seemed to vanish. I have faith in you like I have faith in myself. I put my trust in our love and tested it in my mind.

Guess what? It's strong and it'll last. That makes me happy. It makes the long separation and loneliness seem worthwhile. It's like I'm paying for the rest of our lives of happiness with a year over here. You're doing the same thing. You're having to pay for something you want. I'm paying in days and nights but it's worth every second, minute and hour I lie in this bunk and feel lonely and depressed.

When I get down, I try to see you smiling or laughing or any of the many things you do. The thing I believe I miss the most is waking up in the morning and finding you asleep in the crook of my arm. Maybe I talk too much.

Do you get sick of hearing this trash from me? I don't mean it's trash, but this sentimental stuff. Do I sound like a kid or something? I'm not ashamed of the things I say because I feel all of it or I wouldn't write it. But if it depresses you or makes you sore, I'll stop it. The whole point I try to express is that I love you more than life itself. I'm not good at expressing anything but I'm trying.

Tell me about your job and all about you. Also, send me a picture of you in a frame. Ok? Also, there are some things I could use if you wouldn't mind sending them. Whenever you can send them is fine.

(1) My tennis shoes

(2) Electric coffee pot like we got when we got home.

(3) My cut off short

(4) My baseball-glove

(5) A new Picture of you in a frame (we can't get frames)

(6) This is hard but talk to Theresa and see if she can make a drawing of you (face and hair) and make it like a paint your picture thing with 365 places to color. So, I can color in a square a day. Think that is possible?

There's some more stuff but I can't think now. Oh yeah, that little lamp we bout in Mass. Stuff is hard to get here. It's the last place to get supplies. So most of the stuff is gone before it gets here. This is Phu Bai. Where Dan was. Officially it's called the 8th RRFS. My address is:

SP4 Loren F. Henderson Jr.

XXX-XX-XXXX

8th RRFS, Box 811

APO 96308

Pass it on to whoever wants it. Tell everyone I'll write one of these days if the _ _ _ _ Army will leave me alone for long enough.

Darling, I love you, you know that? I miss you very much. I want you to know I love you very much. Be good and be happy. "Our day will come".

All my love forever.

Your husband,

Frank

P.S. Tell Candy and Hobo (Homer) and Ebony,
"Hello" from Daddy. Boy, I'm making myself sick. Ugh!
P.S.P.S. I'm sending $250 from January pay.

Of course, Frank did not sound like a kid to me. I loved the way he was telling me he loved me.

Frank knew how much I loved him and depended on one him. Also, he loved and depended on me. It had been just the two of us together out in the world for over two years. Now the fear of being so far away from me and not being able to reach out to hold and comfort me had his mind confused.

Frank was my heart and soul. I could not live without him, so after reading his letters, I knew that it was my job to make sure that he was comforted and assured that I could never be anyone else's but his.

The next letter Frank is settling into more of a routine.

January 27, 1971, 2200
Dear Lou,

I love you. Did you know that? If you didn't you do now. How's every little thing? Fine, I hope. You miss me yet? HA! I seem to be writing like you. Well, I guess that happens after you live with someone too long. HAHA. More like not long enough. Well, Uncle Sammy is going to give us a break in 11 months 20 days and let us live together. Isn't he nice?

Oh, before I forget, I'll be sending that money soon as I can get to the APO. I usually don't get through with NAP (Newly Arrived Personnel) training until 5:00 p.m. and the gate to the off-post closes at 4:30 p.m., so I can't make it. The APO, PX, Finance, and other things that you have to go to so often are out of our perimeter and we can't get off before 9:00 a.m. or after 4:30 p.m.

I've been going to the movies (they're free) and the craft shop and to the service club with Lee every night. I've found the craft shop interesting and I'm planning on building or making some things. We go to the Service club for coffee and a place to get library books and read. The movies are free, but the film is usually busted, they have to change reels, places are cut, sometimes they don't have the last reel, have to bring your own chairs, and anything else that could possibly be had, but it usually takes about 2 hours and it kills time.

All this doesn't sound like me, does it? Well, it is. I still like an occasional beer but not very often and I don't drink liquor. Shock, Shock!!! I don't play cards or talk or think of other women. Shock again!! You probably think I've gone off the deep end. Well no.

First, I love my wife very much and I need no crutches to help me along. The thought of you and my love for you is more than a crutch. It's like an invisible power. If I feel down, I think of you and that pulls me through in a matter of seconds. Like I said before, I've changed and it's for the good. I promise you. By no means am I a saint or a holy roller churchgoer. But I'm a devoted husband. Don't worry, I'm not a boring old fool. I'm the same but I've changed. Make sense? I can't explain it, but I'm thoroughly convinced that you'll love me more.

Now that I've got you confused, disappointed, or excited, I'd better go. I love you very, very, much. Be good and I'll see you soon.

Your Hubby,
Frank
P.S. 11 months and 20 days (or less) DLITA

Frank was trying so hard to convince me that he could be a better husband, but he was already the best husband and I loved him just the way he was.

Did we ever argue? Yes, but it never lasted long because we always ended up laughing then making up. Sometimes I think the making-up part was the only reason we argued.

My only concern was that Frank come home to me alive, so I could hold him in my arms again and tell him how much I loved him.

Frank was still a week and days away from getting a letter from me. I am writing every day but will not receive his address until at least January 31st then I can mail all my letters to him, but he will not get them until February.

About the Author

NANCY LOU HENDERSON was born and raised in Texas, where she met and married her soulmate, Frank, when they were both eighteen years old. Since Frank was in the Army when they married, they lived in Massachusetts then Okinawa before Frank went to Vietnam in 1971. After twenty-nine years of marriage at the age of forty-seven, Nancy became a forever widow in 1997 and has continued to be devoted to her soulmate. At age sixty-five and after a prayer to God for a renewal of purpose, her prayer was answered in a dream that sent her to a cedar chest containing a box of letters that would be her inspiration to write a memoir of her life.

Made in the
USA
Lexington, KY